Received On

JAN 1 9 2021

PRAISE FOR THE AUTHORS

DYLAN HOWARD

"The king of Hollywood scoops . . . his work straddles celebrity voyeurism and keen journalism."

—Michael Ware, former Time *&* CNN *war correspondent*

"When Dylan Howard focuses his attention to investigating a case, you can be sure he will uncover sensational new information that we, as readers, viewers or listeners, will find astonishing."

—Dr. Drew Pinsky, New York Times *bestselling author and TV and radio personality*

"Dylan Howard is the rare combination of cutting-edge journalist, true crime commentator, and relentless investigator. Howard passionately brings comprehensive and groundbreaking analysis to the most compelling mysteries of our time."

—Dr. Phil McGraw, host of TV's #1 daytime talk show, Dr. Phil

"Dylan Howard follows every intricate angle of a story and exposes the truth. As a former detective, I know firsthand the skills that make an exceptional investigator and Dylan has them in spades."

—Bo Dietl, former NYPD homicide detective

***

MELISSA CRONIN

"Melissa is one of the most talented, hardworking journalists I've ever had the pleasure to work with."

—Richard Johnson, Page Six, New York Post

"Best investigative reporting on the Kardashian imperium."

—James Wolcott, Vanity Fair

"Melissa Cronin is one of the most talented investigative reporters in history. Her relentless pursuit of the truth has helped crack the most confounding mysteries of our time. She's a star—her work is just awe-inspiring."

—Dibs Baer, former Executive Editor, In Touch *magazine*

***

JAMES ROBERSTON

"James Robertson has spent the last three years fighting the FBI in court to release their Epstein files. His lawsuit may be the best hope for the public to find out what actually happened, and I am honored to represent him."

—*Dan Novack, First Amendment attorney*

"James Robertson's meteoric rise in tabloid and investigative journalism has been nothing short of spectacular. His refusal to give up on a story—no matter how impossible it may seem to crack—is why he's one of the best and someone you can trust."

—*Dan Wootton, Executive Editor of* The Sun

"James Robertson is in a league of his own."

—*Matt Zimmerman, former Senior V.P.,* News & Entertainment Bookings at NBC News

***

PRAISE FOR THE PODCAST *EPSTEIN: DEVIL IN THE DARKNESS*

"*Epstein: Devil in the Darkness* takes a deep dive into Jeffrey Epstein's crimes . . . not to be missed."

—Daily Mail TV

"*Devil in the Darkness* touts exclusive interviews with Epstein's cellmate—who witnessed his first suicide attempt—and, his former chauffeur."

—Vanity Fair

"The twelve-part *Epstein: Devil in the Darkness* has certainly assembled some interesting contributors. . . . There is interesting insight into Epstein's inferiority complex, apparently caused by his failure to finish two separate degree courses, and his relationship with the heiress Ghislaine Maxwell."

—Financial Times

EPSTEIN:

DEAD MEN TELL NO TALES

Other books by Dylan Howard

Diana: Case Solved (2019)

Aaron Hernandez's Killing Fields (2019)

The Last Charles Manson Tapes: Evil Lives Beyond the Grave (2019)

Other Podcasts by the Authors

Fatal Voyage: The Mysterious Death of Natalie Wood

Fatal Voyage: Diana, Case Solved

The Killing of Marilyn Monroe

EPSTEIN:

DEAD MEN TELL NO TALES

SPIES, LIES & BLACKMAIL

DYLAN HOWARD, MELISSA CRONIN & JAMES ROBERTSON

with additional reporting and research by
Katy Forrester, Andy Tillett, and Aaron Tinney

This book is based on new evidence from the explosive
hit podcast *Epstein: Devil in the Darkness*

Skyhorse Publishing

Skyhorse Publishing books may be purchased in bulk at special discounts for sales promotion, corporate gifts, fund-raising, or educational purposes. Special editions can also be created to specifications. For details, contact the Special Sales Department, Skyhorse Publishing, 307 West 36th Street, 11th Floor, New York, NY 10018 or info@skyhorsepublishing.com.

Skyhorse® and Skyhorse Publishing® are registered trademarks of Skyhorse Publishing, Inc.®, a Delaware corporation.

Visit our website at www.skyhorsepublishing.com.

10 9 8 7 6 5 4 3 2

Library of Congress Cataloging-in-Publication Data is available on file.

Cover design by 5mediadesign
Cover photo credit: The Mega Agency

Print ISBN: 978-1-5107-5792-9
eBook ISBN: 978-1-5107-5823-0

Printed in the United States of America

CONTENTS

"I've known Jeff for 15 years. Terrific guy. A lot of fun to be with. He's even said to love beautiful women as much as I do, and many of them are on the younger side."

—Donald Trump, 2002

"I was told Epstein 'belonged to intelligence' and to leave it alone."

—Alex Acosta, former US Attorney in Miami

AUTHORS' NOTE

For investigative reporters, all too often the search for truth stops short before any satisfying conclusion. Leads turn cold and paths of inquiry hit dead ends. In the case of Jeffrey Epstein, even in death, the rabbit hole spirals ever downward, proving to be infinitesimally profound and complex.

Disturbing questions about the convicted pedophile first surfaced on a national scale back in 2008, when Epstein received a sentence of just eighteen months in prison—and that, with work release—following the Palm Beach Police Department's discovery of more than thirty of his teen sex abuse victims.

Former US Labor Secretary Alex Acosta had helped prosecute Epstein at the time, and in the face of critiques, Acosta steadfastly insisted he had simply secured the best deal possible. But when pressed as to whether Epstein had scored a lighter sentence because he was a member of international intelligence, Acosta offered a non-denial denial—in classic politician form.

"This was a case that was brought by our office, it was brought based on the facts and I look at the reporting and others, I can't address it directly because of our guidelines, but I can tell you that a lot of reporting is going down rabbit holes," said Acosta.

Now, through the looking glass of a dogged and extraordinary investigation, we have discovered that the rabbit hole goes deeper than anyone ever could have expected. The world has known only half of the sordid saga that is the life and death of billionaire pedophile Jeffrey Epstein.

Until now.

Dead men like Epstein tell no tales, but we can. In this book, we'll tell a tale of sex victims, dead bodies, spies, death threats, and an international conspiracy the likes of which we have never seen before.

Everyone knows that Epstein used his mathematical genius and ruthless ambition to slither into high society, where he posed as a billionaire investor and charming philanthropist.

His mysterious riches, gaudy private jet, and impenetrable mansion fortresses allowed him to unleash his insatiable appetite for underage girls with impunity for decades. That is beyond dispute.

Now for the first time, however, this unprecedented examination sheds light on an even shadier side of Epstein's dark and twisted life, a story that traverses the globe from the White House, to Manhattan, through New Mexico, Palm Beach, Paris, the US Virgin Islands, and the Israeli Mossad, ending at the Kremlin in Russia.

***

Epstein, at least on the surface, was once the epitome of a jet-setting bachelor. The secretive self-made man who rose from blue-collar Brooklyn to the heights of luxury was a close confidant of presidents, prime ministers, A-list movie stars, and even British royalty.

But for years, there were disturbing whispers that the enigmatic billionaire was secretly running an underground sex-trafficking ring—pimping out the young girls under his control to the richest and most influential men in the world.

Epstein and his powerful pals didn't do much to hide their perversions.

Whether on his private jet, dubbed the "Lolita Express," at his mansions around the world, or on his own private island, Epstein traveled with a roster of young women by his side. For those men invited to join him, it was a global pedophile playground.

Yet these weren't periodic seedy sexcapades. The horrors orchestrated by Epstein were carried out on a daily basis.

A massive police investigation in Florida ended with a whimper in 2007. After just a few months in jail, Epstein was back at it again, flaunting his freedom and his debauchery around the world for more than a decade.

In the summer of 2019, though, the possibility of justice at last seemed real as federal agents officially charged Epstein with organizing the most extensive child sex ring in history.

Some of his brave victims—now adult women—came forward to break their silence and confront their abuser. It seemed his sickest misdeeds would finally be revealed, and those who took part in the corrupt conspiracy would be thrust into the spotlight.

The public was poised to finally learn the awful truth, and to hold all those involved accountable.

But hopes for long-overdue justice were shattered on August 10 when Epstein was found dead in his cell at the Metropolitan Correctional Center in New York City.

The verdict: suicide.

The timing: convenient, to say the least.

The man at the center of the monstrous scheme, the devil who might have finally confessed to save what was left of his soul, was forever silenced.

With no one else charged in the indictment, the criminal case against Epstein himself was dropped. There would be no public trial and no further firsthand evidence unleashed. It seemed that Epstein had ultimately escaped criminal punishment and had silenced his victims yet again.

But that story is not over.

***

For the past eight years, this team of investigators has followed the trail of Epstein's darkest secrets, wherever they led. We conducted dozens of hours of interviews with those who knew Epstein best, secured previously unreleased documents under Freedom of Information Act laws, uncovered and questioned new victims and witnesses—including his onetime chauffeur and his New Mexico "massage therapist" recruiter—obtained recordings of a defiant Epstein himself protesting his innocence, and uncovered photos inside his sex dens of sin and onboard his private jet, the Lolita Express.

At times, we faced pushback.

At times, the facts stopped adding up.

That was when we knew we had to dig deeper into Epstein's dark world.

Luckily, in this case the law would aid our efforts to expose him. Many of our previous investigations into the life of Jeffrey Epstein were hamstrung by the simple fact that he was still alive.

When an individual is still living, it can be virtually impossible to obtain police files, deposition audio, sealed court documents, or any evidence related to their case. But when a person dies, this information can finally be made public with little restriction.

This reality is what allowed us to deliver *Epstein: Dead Men Tell No Tales*, an unprecedented probe into his life and death aimed at uncovering the real truth.

The death of inmate 76318–054 allowed us more access into his personal life than ever before. Here, for the first time ever, we have compiled the shocking information that ultimately led to credible leads and disturbing new evidence. We have pieced together the scattered puzzle he left behind.

Through it all, we fought tirelessly with law enforcement officials to unseal documents and obtain clues that might otherwise have been overlooked. We traveled to New York, Florida, Paris, Russia, and New Mexico in search of the truth, leaving no stone unturned as we uncovered an epic drama of crime, wealth, betrayal, and international intrigue.

We did it all for years with one goal in mind.

We sought an answer to the question the whole world has been asking: How—*and why*—did the man that President Donald Trump once called a "terrific guy" become one of the world's most evil criminals? And why was he able to evade *true* justice for so long?

***

The story of Jeffrey Epstein—as the world knows it—is shocking, and tragic. The full and *real* story—as revealed here for the first time—is so scandalous that it raises pressing questions that implicate the world's elite.

How much did Epstein pals President Bill Clinton, Prince Andrew, and President Donald Trump know about Epstein's perversions—and did they take part?

How might they have helped him to continue his abuse, and to escape justice for it?

What responsibility might they have for his sudden, shocking death?

And will we ever know the truth of the sprawling tale of espionage and blackmail at the heart of this scandal?

The answers to these questions—and more—will be revealed through this compelling investigation sitting in your hands.

Be warned, however: Our reporting is, at times, graphic, disturbing, and distressing, as his victims expose the brutal details of living their worst nightmare.

Be prepared: Our findings also will send shock waves through the establishment and the highest levels of the world's watching, waiting glitterati.

Be assured that you will finally learn the definitive facts about how it all came to a brutal end in a grim Manhattan jail cell.

Was Epstein's death suicide—or murder?

If murder, who was behind it?

And most importantly: **who could be next?**

—DYLAN HOWARD, MELISSA CRONIN & JAMES ROBERTSON

CHAPTER 1

AUTOPSY OF A SCANDAL

Far from the hectic pace of central Manhattan, the cab horns and clamor die down as you enter the leafy streets of the Upper East Side.

There, the stately and historic homes stand proud and quiet, decades of history behind their stony gray facades. One seems to hold even more stories than the others. Four buildings combined, it stretches across an entire block, consuming all the streetfront. Gargoyles crouch on the cornices. A thirty-foot wooden door stands impassive and foreboding at the center. Bill Cosby and Woody Allen are among the neighbors. Inside, there is a massive study, one like Sherlock Holmes would inhabit. A towering bookcase lines the back wall, an oil painting—perhaps an Old Master—in the center. Behind that painting, a safe. Inside that safe, hundreds of CDs and DVDs. On those, thousands of files. Photos and videos. Sexual. Showing young girls. Some, with old men.

FBI agents stumbled upon this hidden trove of evil during a massive raid on the $56 million, 21,000-square-foot property, the home of billionaire financier Jeffrey Epstein, on July 6, 2019. Hours before, Epstein had been arrested in New Jersey on charges of sex trafficking.

The files and their disturbing contents were the final legacy of a man who died trying to keep the secrets of a life filled with depravity; what he left behind, testaments to his sins.

That New York fortress was a town house turned torture chamber, filled with oddities such as a painting of former president Bill Clinton in a blue dress and high heels, and a life-sized female doll hanging from a chandelier.

In the rooms that once hosted Manhattan's elite—from Mort Zuckerman to Google cofounder Sergey Brin, magician David Blaine, Donald Trump, Chelsea Handler, Harvey Weinstein, former Clinton presidential aide George Stephanopoulos, Charlie Rose, and journalist Katie Couric—security cameras peered out from every nook and cranny.

Tucked deep inside the house, a dark room was stacked with monitors recording every moment. Close at hand was a printer.

In another hidden room among the seven stories, a massive professional-grade printer loomed in the shadows. On the walls in that hideaway were blown-up photographs of female bodies—their heads and faces cropped out of the frame. Deep in one dark hallway hung a giant blown-up photo of a grinning Epstein carrying a blonde four- or five-year-old girl on his shoulders. He had no children or nieces.

The same day as the New York raid, hundreds of miles away, agents swarmed Epstein's Caribbean island, Little St. James—Little St. Jeff, to locals—and found more chilling relics. Through the window, we saw dozens of orange evidence bags stacked and ready for analysis. More photos of topless girls covered the walls. His mysterious temple—painted in the colors of the Israeli flag—at last, was breached. (Oddly, investigators found buckets of paint, ladders, and scaffolding inside, as if it had been recently renovated.) Still more files were recovered; dozens of secret cameras, discovered.

As fossilized bones sketch the outlines of prehistoric beasts, so too do these remnants of one man's life spin out into fearsome forms upon contemplation.

What purpose would it serve Jeffrey Epstein—a man who had everything—to record and curate the most private moments of others?

The evidence points overwhelmingly to one possibility: blackmail.

In a world of disturbing secrets and deception, Epstein's international web of blackmail was the aspect of his life that he most desperately tried to hide. Was it the one thing that could have truly destroyed it all?

Even more importantly, how was this web of blackmail connected to yet another question hanging over Epstein and his dark legacy: How did he amass a fortune to rival some of the richest individuals in the world?

Epstein was estimated to have been worth roughly $500 million at the time of his death, despite not having any public means of income. Financial documents uncovered in recent weeks show hundreds of millions of dollars flowing into his shady businesses in the US Virgin Islands: Southern Trust and Financial Trust. Local officials had given him an extremely lax tax deal. No one really asked questions.

For Epstein, the money kept rolling in—and out—right up to the end.

Two days before his death was reported, he secretly signed a new will that placed his millions into a trust, forever hiding its movements. Listed as the executors were Darren K. Indyke and Richard D. Kahn, two longtime associates.

Epstein's former colleague Steven Hoffenberg claims that Indyke and Kahn had once been tasked with investigating Epstein's financial misdeeds at investment group Towers Financial in the 1990s, an investigation that ended with Hoffenberg sentenced to twenty years in prison for running a Ponzi scheme that the SEC considered to be one of the largest in history—at least, prior to Bernie Madoff's crimes a decade later. Epstein, however, skipped off scot-free.

Why were those men chosen as executors?

Who really inherited Epstein's trust?

If he really died, why has his fortune not been seized as evidence in the ongoing investigation into his crimes?

Moreover, if no one inherited those millions . . . is it because he's still alive?

If so, where is Jeffrey Epstein?

Will he ever meet justice?

The answers are there, in what Epstein left behind. In his connections, his crimes, his financial dealings and fears, lies the truth.

One of the most disturbing stories in recent memory, Epstein's tale may also be the most complicated. Yet, it is lying right in front of you.

All you have to do is put together the pieces.

CHAPTER 2

THE BIRTH OF A MONSTER

On July 6, 2019, federal agents swarmed a private jet at New Jersey's private Teterboro airport.

As an unsuspecting Jeffrey Epstein walked off the plane, he was apprehended, handcuffed and placed under arrest—for sex trafficking.

The events of that day not only shocked the convicted pedophile, a man who had long evaded justice but also, stunned the world, a world that had thought his reign of lawless horrors would continue forever.

As Epstein descended through the clouds to his ultimate destiny, he surely had no idea what awaited him on the tarmac.

In those final last moments of blissful ignorance, he would have passed over the very place where it all began. Looking from the windows of his plush private jet, once known as the "Lolita Express," Epstein could have looked down upon the tidy streets and neatly appointed homes of Sea Gate, Brooklyn, the quaint middle-class neighborhood in which he was raised.

As he walked those streets decades before, no one ever could have expected what was to come: how high he would rise, how far he would fall, and how thoroughly his life, his reputation, and his circumstances would change.

***

Born on January 20, 1953, Jeffrey Epstein was the cherished first child of school aide Pauline and gardener Seymour.

On the day of his birth, Dwight D. Eisenhower was sworn in as the thirty-fourth president President of the United States, and shared an ominous warning in his inauguration address: "We sense with all our faculties that forces of good and evil are massed and armed and opposed as rarely before in history." How little did he know.

Epstein's parents had married only months earlier, when Pauline was already pregnant with Jeffrey. Both were children of Jewish European immigrants, and many of their family members had been killed in the Holocaust. Nothing in their background could have hinted at the hellish crimes their son would commit.

A year after Jeffrey's birth, his younger brother Mark was born. The two boys were raised in the quiet enclave of Sea Gate.

Epstein's childhood friend Gary Grossberg spoke exclusively to reporter Andy Tillett about his quiet young life with his charming friend, Jeff—and the surprising way his friend's life has turned out.

"Sea Gate was a very, very beautiful, happy family community," Grossberg began. "If you go out to Sea Gate, Coney Island was there, and it was just very, very private. The beach was there, the ocean was there. It was very, very charming, very charming."

He continued:

> It was great. It was wonderful. The Epsteins are just lovely, lovely people. Absolutely the best. No doubt about it. No doubt in my mind. His mother, just the most wonderful woman. In fact, you know something? When I speak to you, I speak to you with his mother's heart. Okay?
>
> You've got to remember this was in the seventies, and life was very different. There was no Internet. There was no high-profile cable TV. There was no media. There was no nonsense. . . .
>
> I was actually close with Mark, his brother, but Jeff was a friend.
>
> We didn't share a lot of time because he was a year older than us, and he was in a different grade. And due to his magnetic personality and well-being, he was in different circles. . . .

He was always a gentleman, always very kind with everyone. And he did a lot of things for a lot of people. . . .

Always did things right. The Epsteins, they're like that. They're good, kind people, whether it's in education, philanthropy, the facilitation of people. They were around people who were doing these types of things.

People are not talking about that. They're only talking about the individuals who were so-called around him. So it's just unfortunate that this particular situation came down and turned into a cancer.

Jeffrey's a very good-looking guy, number one. Very, very talented. He's got money and people, women. They became jealous, whatever it may be. And so I don't believe all these stories about all this nonsense. I'm not saying that there were no improprieties, because who knows, I wasn't there. But I can only tell you about the caliber of the individual that people are talking about. . . .

I only knew and know of the Epsteins in a very, very wonderful way, and it's important for people to speak the truth. And as I say, I don't believe any of these stories about any of that stuff going on because I don't know him that way. I'm telling you the truth. And I'm not trying to hide anything. I'm letting you know exactly. I don't believe it.

I truly believe that this was politically motivated. I guarantee you that he would have never been arrested if Alex Acosta was not on Trump's cabinet. If he wasn't connected, if there was no election, if there was nothing happening . . . it's shit. Everything had happened. It's very sad."

Like most children in the neighborhood, Epstein attended local public schools with Grossberg, later entering the Lafayette High School in South-Central Brooklyn.

Already making his mark, Epstein skipped his freshman and sophomore years, and joined the math team, where he competed with Brenda Solovitz.

In an exclusive interview with our team, Solovitz said Epstein still seemed like a normal guy in high school, too.

> At that time, he seemed to be just like a normal person. I don't know of him doing anything outrageous. He was no worse and no different to the rest of us at that point.
>
> "He probably came to my house as part of the math team. Sometimes I made a lasagna and they'd all come over for lunch, but that was it really.
>
> I don't know what he did, but he seemed normal to us. There was nothing about his behavior that seemed off.
>
> He was really bright, and he was in the honors classes I was in, and certainly we moved in the same classes. He seemed fine, just seemed normal, y'know? He wasn't standoffish from people. He was funny sometimes. He fit right in. He didn't seem like a geek. To me, he seemed like a normal person.
>
> His father worked in the parks department and that wasn't unusual at that time. A lot of us came from lower middle—what used to be middle class, but we lived in housing projects and things like that. It was just our fathers' luck, but we didn't have a lot of money.
>
> To me he was a normal guy, a really bright normal guy.

From there, though, Epstein's path would grow rockier as his dark side began to emerge. In 1969, sixteen-year-old Epstein graduated from high school two years early and entered the prestigious Cooper Union college in lower Manhattan. At Cooper Union, he took advanced math classes and made extra cash by tutoring classmates. But suddenly and inexplicably, he dropped out in spring 1971.

Just a few months later, Epstein enrolled instead at New York University's Courant Institute of Mathematical Sciences, where he studied the mathematical aspects of heart physiology. But in June 1974—when the go-go 1960s had given way to the gas lines and financial downturn of the 1970s—Epstein again quit school, having failed to receive a degree from either institution.

It remains something of a mystery as to why he dropped out of both institutions. Still, the decision to end his academic career would not slow ambitious Epstein's rise through Manhattan's elite.

That fall, the twenty-one-year-old college dropout was hired to teach math and physics at the Dalton School, one of Manhattan's most prestigious private schools. Located on the ritzy Upper East Side, Dalton then cost roughly $3,000 a year to attend—more than $15,000 in modern currency. Today, the annual tuition has ballooned to more than $50,000.

When Epstein arrived, the school was filled with rich kids from the upper echelon that he was desperate to enter. Soon-to-be celebrity students who attended Dalton while Epstein was a teacher included *Dirty Dancing* star Jennifer Grey, Maggie Wheeler (Janice from *Friends*), media mogul Rupert Murdoch's daughter Prudence, and Michael J. Fox's future wife Tracy Pollan, who starred in the 1980s sitcom *Family Ties*.

In an unusual twist of fate, Epstein was hired at the prestigious institution only months after authoritarian headmaster Donald Barr had stepped down. Barr was the father of current US Attorney General William Barr, the man who would later be responsible for prosecuting Epstein, in 2019.

As headmaster, the elder Barr had turned the notoriously progressive school into a punishingly conservative institution. Girls were sent home for wearing short skirts; boys, for having long hair. Teachers were forbidden from wearing casual or eccentric clothes, the colors and cuts that had been fashionable just a few years before. And if students were busted for smoking weed, they could only avoid expulsion by undergoing therapy. Barr was the Dalton dictator, and he considered his orders "ukases"—an Imperial Russian term for edicts made by a czar.

"They think they can cheat on tests, steal from one another's lockers and exploit each other emotionally so long as they have the right opinions about the war or civil rights or something else," Barr said at the time. "That is not morality."

Halfway through the 1974 school year, the conservative headmaster clashed with the Dalton board of trustees and resigned in protest. His replacement, Dr. Gardner Dunnan, rolled back some of the stricter codes of conduct, giving Epstein—a predator in the making—the perfect hunting ground.

With no outdoor hangout areas, students socialized in the hallways, and Epstein frequently inserted himself into these groups. At the time, most students viewed him as a quirky young teacher who cared more about gossiping than grading.

"I won't say that the girls didn't like him, but they thought he was odd," former Dalton alumna Karin Williams said of the young teacher. "You noticed him. He stood out as this young guy in this weird coat."

(Williams is referring to the full-length fur coat Epstein wore to school, the kind favored by the men who lorded over the streetwalkers off Times Square, or who waited at Penn Station to swoop in on fresh-faced new arrivals to the city.)

Under that coat, Epstein kept the top two buttons of his shirt open, exposing a gold chain necklace. Most girls didn't take him seriously, and perhaps that was precisely how Epstein wanted them to think of him: laid-back and approachable.

"I was a 14-year-old and he helped me through a time when there wasn't anybody else to talk to," Dalton graduate Leslie Kitziger told the *New York Times* in a 2019 exposé on Epstein's Dalton years. "He listened . . . I felt like he really cared that I was having a rough go."

Former student Scott Spizer even remembered Epstein popping up at a boozy student party, and recalled the special attention he gave to the girls.

"I can remember thinking at the time, 'This is wrong,'" Spizer told the *Times*. "He was much more present amongst the students, specifically the girl students, during non-teaching hours. . . . It was kind of inappropriate."

What's more, Dalton alumnus Mark Robinson claimed that Epstein wasn't the only faculty member cruising the halls for sexual conquests.

"There were a number of teachers who looked at the student body as their next meal," Robinson alleged.

But Epstein didn't get far. Amid complaints about his lackadaisical teaching style, the Dalton school board terminated Epstein after the 1976 school year.

"It was determined that he had not adequately grown as a new teacher to the standard of the school," said Peter Branch, head of the high school at the time. Branch only recalled getting complaints about Epstein's poor academic abilities, though—not his personal habits.

True to form, Epstein somehow managed to turn that failure into a stepping-stone to even greater success: a job on Wall Street.

During a parent-teacher conference, the twenty-three-year-old had managed to dazzle one student's financier father. So, when Epstein was fired from Dalton, the broker connected Epstein with Alan Greenberg, a Wall Street bigwig who was poised to become chief executive officer of multibillion-dollar global investment bank and brokerage firm Bear Stearns.

"This parent was so wowed by the conversation he told my father, 'You've got to hire this guy,'" Greenberg's daughter Lynne Koeppel recalled to the *Miami Herald*. "That was Jeff. He was very smart and he knew how to woo people, how to schmooze . . . If that was his plan, it worked."

Later that year, Epstein landed a job at Bear Stearns as a low-level junior assistant to a floor trader. He swiftly rose through the ranks, and within four years he had become a limited partner, taking on mega-millionaire clients like Seagram president Edgar Bronfman. For Epstein, it was a boyhood dream come true. But it wouldn't last.

CHAPTER 3

FOLLOW THE MONEY

By 1980, Jeffrey Epstein's life was a fast-paced collage of frantic days on Wall Street and glittering nights among Manhattan's elite. He had managed to climb into yet another exclusive circle of society, and for the first time—it must have seemed—nothing was off limits.

As he began his finance career, Epstein was heralded as an uncommon genius from the start, chosen personally by Wall Street icon Alan Greenberg to be his protégé. (Greenberg served as Bear Stearns' CEO from 1978 to 1993 and as chairman of the board from 1985 to 2001. He also served as a non-executive director of Viacom.)

"Bear Stearns never had any training program," Epstein said in a recently unsealed interview we obtained. "There was no course to begin. Alan Greenberg said he wanted me to learn each area of the business.

"He thought the best place for me to start would be on the floor of the American Stock Exchange and then later move up to the trading desk and learn all the different areas of the firm, including the margin department. He was amazing."

But in less than a year, Epstein found his niche. He analyzed the portfolios of wealthy clients and came up with cunning money-saving schemes.

Getting in on Wall Street before the 1980s banking boom allowed Epstein to build a spectacular network of connections that made him the toast of Manhattan during one of the most prosperous decades it had ever seen. In just a few short years with Bear Stearns, Epstein had made millions of dollars, was traveling full-time by chauffeured limo, had billionaires relying on his financial advice, and was carousing around town with stunning women on both arms.

A close friend from that period, *Vanity Fair* contributing author Jesse Kornbluth, recalled how Epstein became a rising star of the social scene in an exclusive interview with investigative reporter Andy Tillett, who contributed to this book.

> I would say Jeffrey Epstein's money, how much there is, how he got it, is a complete mystery, and not just to me.
>
> I met Jeffrey Epstein in 1987, at a party given by Pepsi-Cola. He was with a blue jeans manufacturer. We chatted, and he seemed interesting. We decided we'd carry on this conversation again elsewhere.
>
> Jeffrey was Peter Pan. He looked young, was fit, cheerful, and self-amused. . . . He had an ironic smile, which is congenial to me, since I find a lot of things ironic as well. I guess the final thing to say is, New York was not then, because of the huge interest in finance, populated by very interesting heterosexual men. There were many interesting gay men, but heterosexual men doing business, not so much. Jeffrey was one of the few.
>
> New York's the big leagues. You've got to be *good* to do it here, at the level of a Madoff, or an Epstein. He actually seemed not just smart, but accomplished. Those are very attractive qualities, and he was unmarried, so he was the ideal extra man. He was invited places. He made his way rather quickly. There was nothing about him of the freak and pervert that he would come to be.

Still, Kornbluth said, when he got to know Epstein more intimately, the whiz kid's carefully constructed façade began to crack.

> Brighter minds than I say that he had actually really very little ability. That his mind skittered. That when the conversation

turned serious, he made an ironic joke and changed it. This makes it incredibly puzzling that, say, someone like Leon Black, a major financier with a large, large department of tax experts, would say, "Jeffrey, you'll be my tax adviser." These sorts of things make no sense. As for his education, we know there was none. He came from Brooklyn, was a high school graduate. His parents weren't distinguished in any way.

Harry Evans once described his wife, Tina Brown, as being cunning like a desert rat. That was a compliment. I think Epstein was, too. He had enough knowledge that he could talk for five minutes about anything, and for six minutes about none.

I had no reason to disbelieve his fantastic stories. I was not then a novelist. On the other hand, I was interested in confirming.

He sometimes helped dictators hide their money. He sometimes helped Americans recover the money that dictators had. It seemed cheerfully amoral, and that is what interested me and make me want to write about him. I said, "Jeffrey, let me see you work."

I saw him in two places. One, he had this vast office that used to be at Random House. It was largely empty, and you couldn't tell what work was being done there.

Another time, we arranged to meet in the lobby of a Park Avenue building, and we took the elevator up to a law office, where Jeffrey was going to serve a subpoena. He didn't get past the receptionist, and I found the whole event puzzling. On the one hand, you're recovering millions and millions of dollars. On the other hand, you're doing what a process server does.

Those incidents rattled Kornbluth, and he began to doubt if Epstein really was the man he claimed to be. But there was one disturbing interaction that truly ended their relationship once and for all.

I was about to be married to an extremely beautiful historian, who had just published a book of military history.

The night before we were to be married, we had separate phones, and he called her on hers and said, "Since you're going to be married tomorrow, this is your last night of freedom. Why don't you can come over and sleep with me?" At first, she didn't take it seriously. It was just the sort of flip thing that any number of friends would have said. But no, he was actually serious. That was a major tell.

Then, a few days later, days after our marriage, someone purporting to be me called a number of women, including some of our friends saying, "It's Jesse Kornbluth. I'd love to go out with you." They called us to say, "Somebody, Jesse, is impersonating you." Who would do that?

My wife's theory is, "It had to be Jeffrey."

Meanwhile, Epstein was growing ever more desperate—and reckless—in his pursuit of money and influence.

In early 1981, one of Epstein's colleagues at Bear Stearns tipped off management that Epstein was testing the boundaries of the law. After an investigation, Epstein admitted he had loaned $20,000 to a friend, Warren Eisenstein, who then used the money to invest in stocks, with Epstein's insider knowledge guiding him. It was unethical, and potentially illegal. Epstein wasn't fired, but he was fined $2,500 and passed over for a partner promotion.

That was humiliating in itself, but a few days after that there was an even more painful blow. The US Securities and Exchange Commission (SEC) opened an investigation into Epstein's client Edgar Bronfman, and Epstein was accused of illegal securities violations.

Depending on who you ask, Epstein was either unceremoniously fired at that point, or quit in a blaze of glory. Either way, it left the unabashed social climber in a very undesirable position.

No longer a Wall Street wunderkind, Epstein was jobless, homeless, and running out of funds. He had to get creative.

Desperate Epstein bent the rules even further and began taking on controversial black-market clients, like Saudi Arabian businessman Adnan Khashoggi, the man who had been implicated when the Iran-Contra Affair became public in 1986.

(The Iran-Contra Affair was a secret US arms deal in 1985 that traded missiles and other arms to Iran. Officially, the deal was struck to free Americans hostages held by terrorists in Lebanon. Secretly, however, the American government had sold the weapons and used the proceeds to support armed conflict in Nicaragua. The controversial scheme—and the ensuing political scandal—threatened to bring down the presidency of Ronald Reagan. The hub of much of the Contra activity was in Arkansas, while Bill Clinton was governor.)

Epstein's involvement was to help Khashoggi broker global armament deals, which was more than just old guns in crates; it included the sale of major weaponry like the AWACS (Airborne Warning and Control System) aircraft.

Meanwhile, according to a US Defense Intelligence Agency report, Khashoggi was also one of the biggest drug traffickers doing business in Colombia in the 1980s and 1990s.

But Adnan Khashoggi was not only an arms dealer; he also worked with and for the CIA. During this period, Epstein was known to boast that he was a CIA agent as well. Khashoggi was not his only link. Epstein's old Dalton connection Donald Barr had worked for the OSS before becoming a headmaster. Barr's son William Barr would later work for the CIA as well.

After Epstein's death, the FBI would find he'd used an Austrian passport with a fake name to enter the United Kingdom, Saudi Arabia, and Spain during that period. His lawyers have insisted it was to avoid an anti-Semitic attack—not to avoid the attention of the authorities in the United States.

Despite his growing social network, Epstein certainly was spiraling further and further away from the exclusive circles of proper society that he'd always wanted to inhabit.

Then in 1987, he got what seemed like a lucky break, meeting Steven Hoffenberg of Tower Financial Corporation, a leading debt collection and corporate raiding agency at the time. Hoffenberg recalled that heady period in a series of exclusive interviews with our team.

"Towers Financial was a publicly traded company involved in accounts receivable collection and financing and asset financing and was raising money on Wall Street in the capital markets," Hoffenberg told reporter Doug Montero.

> Jeffrey Epstein applied to Towers Financial for a position in investment banking via an introduction from his employer in Europe named Douglas Leese who was very unhappy with Jeffrey Epstein's behavior. . . . Epstein submitted expenses for hundreds of thousands of dollars that were inappropriate. They wanted to discharge Jeffrey Epstein.
>
> They realized, though, that he had a great ability on Wall Street and this company was partners overseas with Towers Financial. They asked me if I would interview him and consider him for the investment banking division of Towers Financial. That's what occurred. That's how I met him.
>
> The time frame of our first meeting in New York City at Towers Financial's headquarters was in the eighties, probably more like '86, '87. Jeffrey Epstein had worked in Europe. . . . He was very heavily involved in the illegal side of the business, of the money laundering, the spying, the arms sales. I'm sure there was some legitimate components that wouldn't be criminal, but the majority of his work product was criminal.
>
> At this late hour of many years later, I like being concise and I don't want to misquote, but I can tell you that they sold armament throughout the Middle East and around the world. There was a sale of aircraft, I believe. The AWACS or the air force protective planes for spying, they were involved in that . . . and they

were involved in all types of armament being sold. They did work a partnership with Adnan Khashoggi's group in Saudi Arabia regularly and selling armament with Adnan Khashoggi's folks in Saudi Arabia and throughout the Middle East.

Nevertheless, Hoffenberg said:

I was very impressed with the unbelievable personality and unbelievable ability of Jeffrey Epstein to become a friend and the uncanny ability that he had as a mastermind criminal on Wall Street.

Jeffrey Epstein was a brilliant, brilliant Wall Street mastermind in criminality for securities fraud. I was greatly impressed with his demeanor, his ability to understand complex securities underwritings and sales to investors. He was also broke. He was literally without funds because he got into trouble in Europe and had gotten into trouble at Bear Stearns.

He was extraordinarily gifted. Very talented, very personable, very able to get to be liked at once by people, and a mastermind of criminality on Wall Street. He was so unusual as an executive and had so much ability. It was just very surprising how gifted he was.

His ability to sell you securities when you weren't looking to acquire securities was remarkable. He would end up convincing you to buy securities in Towers Financial and you weren't even considering that. He had that gift and that ability.

He was a master manipulator.

But Epstein's manipulations weren't always done through legal means. By the early nineties, the authorities had set their sights on Towers—and Epstein—for operating a multimillion-dollar Ponzi scheme.

Hoffenberg explained:

> The securities violations at Towers Financial was branded as a Ponzi crime. You raise money from one investor to pay another investor. That's the simple definition of Ponzi. Jeffrey Epstein participated full time and was a mastermind in that part of the Towers Financial crimes.
>
> Towers Financial got into an awful lot of legal problems and litigations and ended up going into bankruptcy. Trustees were appointed to operate the company . . .
>
> Jeffrey Epstein had a very strong relationship with the lawyers that the trustee hired. Actually, the trustee in bankruptcy at Towers Financial, a man named Alan Cohen, hired one of Jeffrey Epstein's best friends and lawyers, Indyke and Kahn, to investigate Jeffrey Epstein at Towers Financial, which is remarkable.
>
> Jeffrey Epstein manipulated that occurrence without question. Absolutely, it was a brilliant manipulation, shockingly.

The outcome was just as jaw-dropping.

"Epstein was not punished in the crimes at Towers Financial," Hoffenberg said. "Jeffrey Epstein's ability as a master criminal got him out of the penalty box for all of that. That's what happened continuously in his other criminal charges as well."

Hoffenberg, meanwhile, was sentenced to twenty years in prison, a $1 million fine, and $463 million in restitution.

Epstein didn't just escape justice, however. Hoffenberg claimed he moved on to new adventures—with millions in his pocket.

"Epstein was able to fund his criminal enterprise Financial Trust Company and J. Epstein and Company," Hoffenberg alleged. "There was another. I believe it was International Asset Collections. He was able to fund it with the assets and money from the Towers Financial crimes."

Meanwhile, Epstein did have one reputable high-profile client: Les Wexner, founder and CEO of The Limited, a company that includes the lingerie empire Victoria's Secret. Epstein first crossed paths with the billionaire business tycoon in Palm Beach in the mid-1980s. Epstein reportedly stopped Wexner from investing in the stock market shortly before the 1987 crash, and as a result, Epstein and Wexner became very close, very fast.

"They had a very deep bond, a very deep friendship and a very deep business relationship for a number of years," explained Hoffenberg.

Epstein took a hands-on approach to cleaning up Wexner's vast holdings. He unloaded bad investments, tightened Wexner's budgets, streamlined his profitable assets, and even fired deadweight.

By all accounts, Wexner was impressed—and grateful.

At the time Epstein began working with Wexner, the State Department was his landlord. According to property records, Epstein rented a posh apartment from the State Department at 34 E 69th Street from 1992 to 1995, for the cool sum of $15,000 per month. The home featured carved oak doors, a white marble foyer, a book-stacked library, a marble central staircase, antique furnishings throughout, and—perfect for Epstein—a steam room.

Life for Epstein was good, but Wexner could make it even better.

In 1989, Wexner had purchased the 40-room Herbert N. Straus Mansion at Manhattan's 9 E 71st Street for a cool $13.2 million. At the time, it was the highest-ever recorded residential real estate sale. The fifty-two-year-old completely gutted and renovated the interior of the 1933 stone masterpiece. He also added security cameras, closed-circuit TVs, telephones, and heated sidewalks to melt the snow.

When the renovation was finished, Wexner gave it to Jeffrey Epstein. On January 11, 1996, *The New York Times* reported, "Reached in Florida last week, Epstein said the house was now his."

The way that Epstein became lord of that manor has always been something of a mystery. Strangely, that initial property transaction was never recorded in New York City records online. When Epstein transferred the property between two of his own shell companies in 2011, property records recorded no original purchase price. Highly unusual, the document indicates that when Epstein acquired the home from Wexner, the transaction did not involve money.

The following year in Palm Beach, Florida, Epstein purchased a 14,000-square-foot residence on posh El Brillo Way for $2.5 million, not far from Trump's sprawling Mar-a-Lago estate.

For the first time in a decade, Epstein was back on top. Still, there was further he could go.

In 1991, Epstein convinced Wexner to give him full power of attorney over his business affairs.

"People have said it's like we have one brain between the two of us," Epstein said at the time. "Each has a side."

As for Wexner, he said of Epstein, "I think we both possess the skill of seeing patterns. Jeffrey sees patterns in politics and financial markets, and I see patterns in lifestyle and fashion trends."

"He is always a most loyal friend," Wexner continued. "He does not pick a fight, but if there is a fight, he will let you choose your weapon."

Epstein's friendship with Wexner won him some legitimacy among the business world's elite, but the stories of his sleazy backroom dealings continued. Stuart Pivar, an art collector who was also friends with Epstein at the time, told reporter Andy Tillett that Epstein's ability to spin the truth was unsurpassed.

"He ruined a lot of people commercially from doing all kinds of terrible rotten deals, because he was basically a terrible, bad man," Pivar said. "He outgrew his normalcy, let's put it that way. Jeffrey did things that people don't do.

"He liked to fool people. When you walked in [to his apartment] there was a huge Max Beckmann and I went over and said, 'Jeffrey, wow, that's magnificent!' He said, 'That's a fake!'

"He had fooled me and he liked the idea. He likes to fool.

"Jeffrey would make things up you know, believe it or not. Why did he do that? Just as a game. He liked to keep things interesting . . . a form of practical joke that people don't do. But Jeffrey did things that people don't do."

In those early days, some questioned whether Epstein's life of glamour and intrigue was as tenuous as the 1980s financial boom that went bust.

Laura Goldman mingled with Wall Streeters during that period, and told reporter Marc Lupo that it was clear that no matter how Epstein tried, he didn't quite fit in.

"Well, I had some questions when I met Jeffrey Epstein. Of course, he said he was a hedge fund billionaire. But I had some doubts about that because I went to Wharton with some of the leading investors on Wall Street 'til this day. Went to school with Steve Cohen, Gotham Securities, Joel Greenblatt, and none of them were doing business with him.

"I said to myself, 'Well, these are some of the greatest investors of all time and Jeffrey Epstein doesn't have money with them. So does he have as much money as he says?'"

In any case, it was clear that money wouldn't be enough to get Epstein where he wanted to go. He needed something else.

CHAPTER 4

LADY GHISLAINE

Jeffrey Epstein continued his messy rise through the ranks of New York society. Across the ocean, British publishing magnate and aristocrat Robert Maxwell was coming to the end of the line.

The two men—separated by several time zones and a few decades in age—could have been friends in another life.

Both had risen from humble circumstances to the heights of the elite. While Epstein's parents lived among Holocaust survivors, Maxwell and his family had fled the Nazis, moving to England from Czechoslovakia before World War II began. Maxwell then served with the exiled Czechoslovak Army, fought on the beach at Normandy, and parlayed his fame as a war hero into a publishing empire. Later an elected Member of Parliament, Maxwell traveled over land by helicopter, and by water in his 180-foot yacht *Lady Ghislaine*—named for his beloved youngest daughter.

That yacht would ultimately take him to his watery grave.

At 4:45 a.m. on November 5, 1991, just off the coast of the Canary Islands, Maxwell calmly radioed the members of the *Lady Ghislaine* crew to lower the heat in his cabin. It was his final order. Just a few hours later, fishermen found the tycoon's naked body floating in the North Atlantic.

At the time of his death, no one knew that Maxwell's businesses were on the precipitous edge of collapse. Within weeks of his demise, a $560-million-dollar hole was discovered in the pension funds of his companies. An embezzler of almost unimaginable scale, he had illegally raided the funds to prop up his empire. As *The Guardian* noted, when the full extent of his crimes was uncovered, fawning headlines such as "The Man Who Saved *The Mirror*" were swiftly replaced by epithets like "Maxwell: The Robber."

When it comes to the official verdict on how Maxwell died, opinions remain mixed. One conclusion: heart attack. Another: drowning. Worse still: an assassination.

"He was a man who could not face the ignominy of jail, of being shown to be a liar and a thief—and he very much knew that was coming," Roy Greenslade, a former editor of one of Maxwell's newspapers, the *Daily Mirror*, told *The Guardian*. "So I am a suicide theorist. I believe Maxwell threw himself off."

But Ken Lennox, then the *Mirror*'s senior photographer, who saw the publisher's naked corpse shortly after it was pulled from the sea, is convinced: It was an accident.

"He used to get up at night and pee over the stern of the ship. Everybody knew this. And he weighed about 22 stone [309 pounds] at this time. The railings were wire. So I think he lost his balance, because he was very top-heavy," Lennox said. "He was Teflon man. I don't think he committed suicide."

According to author Martin Dillon, his favorite daughter Ghislaine, then thirty, wasn't buying it either.

"She was the one who felt that he had been murdered," Dillon, author of *Robert Maxwell, Israel's Superspy*, told our team in an exclusive interview.

"Maxwell wasn't the kind of guy who just sort of fell into the water because he was standing in the back of the boat."

So, who did it?

Dillon points to evidence that he claims is clear: "The evidence that Maxwell was working with Mossad is the evidence of people like Rafi Eitan. Rafi Eitan was one of the most famous of all the Mossad agents, so he went on the record to say that Maxwell was an agent—much against the wishes of his former colleagues at Mossad, but he did. And he wasn't the only one. We had some very, very important people make the same claims. Since our book was published, other people have come up with other evidence, and the British knew that Maxwell was working for the Mossad."

Investigative reporter Seymour Hersh also alleged in his book *The Samson Option: Israel's Nuclear Arsenal and American Foreign Policy* that Maxwell was tied to the Israeli Mossad. Hersh was sued for the allegation, but later received an apology.

Even more convincingly, files from the British Foreign Office released in 2003 reveal that British intelligence had reason to believe Maxwell was a spy. In a file titled "Captain Ian Maxwell," a British intelligence officer called the boorish publishing baron "a thoroughly bad character and almost certainly financed by Russia."

Intelligence officer Digby Ackland wrote in one 1959 report, "Capt. Maxwell's questionable activities have been brought to the notice of the Foreign Office on several occasions over the past 10 years."

Maxwell's son Kevin denied that the reports were legit, but Maxwell family friend Laura Goldman insists that the mogul was a double or even triple agent.

"Robert Maxwell traveled in very rarefied circles. He had information about government ministers, about scientific discoveries, about Internet and data information. I think that was valuable to many governments," she told Marc Lupo, a reporter who worked with these authors on *Epstein: Dead Men Tell No Tales*. "My feeling is that he probably was an agent to the Russians, the Israelis, and the British. I believe that Ghislaine continued his work."

According to Dillon's sources, that's a valid belief.

"If I was running Mossad operations I would want Ghislaine Maxwell on my payroll," he said. "I would want her working for us, because she has access to the kind of people whose views are very important in terms of the way in which the world functions."

Soon, Epstein was part of the mix as well. (By 2004, documents obtained by this team reveal, he was the custodian of correspondence and files belonging to Robert Maxwell, which were stored at his Palm Beach home.)

Although it has been reported that he first encountered Ghislaine after her father's death in New York, one insider—a former high-ranking official for the organization that is said to have killed Maxwell—has insisted their connection came far earlier.

Ari Ben-Menashe, a former Israeli spy and alleged "handler" of Robert Maxwell, said of Epstein: "Maxwell introduced him to us, and he wanted us to accept him as part of our group."

Ben-Menashe claimed that Epstein and Ghislaine were already dating in the late 1980s, and that Maxwell Senior grew fond of the young upstart.

"Epstein was hanging around with Robert Maxwell and the daughter was hanging around there too, and that's how they met," he told our team's James Robertson in an interview from Montreal. "Just two young souls, they met."

"Maxwell sort of started liking him, and my theory is that Maxwell felt that this guy is going for his daughter," Ben-Menashe said. "He felt that he could bless him with some work and help him out in like a paternal [way]."

According to the former spy, the ultimate order to embrace Epstein and involve him in the ongoing arms deals came from "the bosses" at Israeli intelligence headquarters.

"They were agents of the Israeli Intelligence Services," he told Robertson.

"Later on [Ghislaine] got involved with Israeli intelligence together with him. But not in this arms deal with Iran business," Ben-Menashe also told Zev Shalev, former CBS News executive producer and investigative journalist for the website *Narativ*.

"These guys were seen as agents. They weren't really competent to do very much. And so they found a niche for themselves—blackmailing American and other political figures."

In closing, Ben-Menashe told Robertson, "Mr. Epstein was the simple idiot who was going around providing girls to all kinds of politicians in the United States. See, fucking around is not a crime. It could be embarrassing, but it's not a crime. But fucking a fourteen-year-old girl is a crime. And he was taking photos of politicians fucking fourteen-year-old girls—if you want to get it straight. They would just blackmail people, they would just blackmail people like that."

***

Even in the early years, the Maxwells surrounded themselves with bold-faced names.

Two years before media magnate Maxwell fell to his death from the *Lady Ghislaine*, he made Donald Trump the guest of honor at a May 1989 bash, we were able to confirm. Also present was Maxwell's cherished daughter Ghislaine.

Did the men compare super-yachts? Maxwell had bought his from Saudi Arabia's Khashoggi family: the relatives of arms dealer Adnan. Trump, meanwhile, had purchased his from Adnan directly—a purchase that was reported the very same year as the Maxwell party, 1989, in *The Superyachts* by Boat International.

Perhaps taking a cue from Maxwell, Trump named his yacht after his daughter as well: *Trump Princess*. Daughter Ivanka was then just eight years of age.

For Trump, the purchase was a strange one. "I'm not into [boats]," he once said. "I've been on friends' boats before and couldn't get off fast enough."

So why make the purchase for nearly $30 million? Whatever the reason, it linked Trump to two of the most powerful—and dangerous—men in the world: Maxwell and Khashoggi. Later, those same connections would lead Trump down a shady path to Epstein.

The Maxwell family's connections were just as strong across the political divide.

According to a 1992 *New York Times* article, then-Governor Bill Clinton's close friend Howard Paster moved from Clinton's gubernatorial campaign to become the head of Hill and Knowlton, a publicity firm representing Maxwell's firm, Maxwell Communication P.L.C. Other clients of Hill & Knowlton included Saudi Arabia, Kuwait, Adnan Khashoggi, and the controversial Bank of Credit and Commerce International.

Ghislaine would later become close friends with the Clinton family, working in conjunction with the Clinton Global Initiative, vacationing on a yacht with Chelsea Clinton in 2009—and even appearing as a guest of honor at Chelsea's 2010 wedding to Marc Mezvinsky.

Had Ghislaine and her father established themselves as Epstein's handlers in order to blackmail prominent Americans, including the Clintons?

In the meantime, Ghislaine and Epstein had their eyes on even more targets.

CHAPTER 5

THE LITTLE BLACK BOOK AND THE LOLITA EXPRESS

"People think intelligence is just about tracking down terrorists, but if you could get into the company of people, former presidents, people who are working on some of the newest software and scientific developments. . . . That's what intelligence really is."
— *Espionage expert Martin Dillon*

When Robert Maxwell died in 1991, Ghislaine hopped a plane and moved to Manhattan. Many people we spoke to believe she was ready to continue her father's legacy. Guaranteed $100,000 a year from her father's trust for the rest of her life, she found easy entrée into Manhattan society and was soon rubbing shoulders with billionaires and beauties in the City of Big Shots. So much so, Maxwell family friend Laura Goldman said that Ghislaine made social climbing her full-time job.

> In the nineties, I spent a lot of time in New York, and I met Ghislaine Maxwell at several parties, openings. Basically, if there was an opening, she was there. She is one of the most intelligent people I met. She's lively, energetic.
>
> I never quite understood what she did for a living, or if she did anything for a living. But she was a nice person.

What people don't understand about the Maxwells, though, is they're very *Upstairs, Downstairs*. If you've seen *Downton Abbey* or other British dramas, they're very upstairs and there's a big separation. I really think she was raised not to worry about the other people. They were a means to an end.

Ghislaine saw something of value, however, in Jeffrey Epstein.

Said Goldman, "Ghislaine Maxwell was nice to every lady in the room. But she only had eyes for one person, and that was Jeffrey."

I think it's kind of apparent that they're kindred souls. I believe that they definitely slept together, I just don't believe they really dated. I think that the connection between them was that he had the cash and she had the connections.

Most of what I know about Ghislaine's relationship with Jeffrey Epstein came from her sister Isabel. Isabel really thought that her sister couldn't quit him, could not quit Jeffrey Epstein. She loved him and wanted to marry him.

When you're someone who's dealt with abuse, you always think if you do one more thing right, that person will marry you, love you, and whatever. He wasn't going to do that. But I really believe that she loved him, she cared for him, and wanted to marry him—and would do anything to make that happen.

Just how far would Ghislaine go?

Seemingly overnight, Ghislaine became Epstein's closest confidante, best friend, and, eventually, something more. Meanwhile, Epstein's new relationship with the European heiress drew the attention of the movers and shakers in the kingdoms of New York and Palm Beach.

With Ghislaine by his side, Epstein had his passport to a whole new world. Now no longer just another flashy Wall Street nouveau riche hopeful, he was beginning to be seen as a serious player with serious influence.

Under Ghislaine's guiding hand, Epstein threw lavish dinner parties with exclusive guest lists at his Upper East Side mansion, and more raucous affairs at his Palm Beach mansion. At first, the purpose of these early dalliances was to win friends and business connections. But darker elements were bubbling beneath the surface.

While Ghislaine and Jeffrey posed happily for the cameras at exclusive events, they went even further to cultivate an inglorious secret social set behind closed doors—on Epstein's private jet, later known as the Lolita Express.

A three-engine 727 jetliner, the Lolita Express was actually a commercial liner retrofitted for personal use. Photos of the interior suggest what kind of use Epstein had in mind.

Plush and carpeted on almost every surface, the jet looked more like a 1970s adult film set than a mode of transportation, as our exclusive photo insert shows.

Rather than individual seats, banquettes lined the wall or curved together in cozy semicircles. The floor was padded.

In the back, there was a suite with a bed and secret shower.

The jet could host twenty-nine people comfortably, but Epstein and Maxwell more frequently hosted intimate affairs in the sky.

Flight logs we obtained in 2015 read like a who's who of early 1990s society. From Hollywood, there were actors Kevin Spacey, comedian Chris Tucker, actor Ralph Fiennes, magician David Blaine, singers Jimmy Buffet and Courtney Love. Media moguls Charlie Rose and Bill Wallace make an appearance. From the world of tech, Bill Gates. Political leaders such as Tony Blair, Ehud Barak, and conservative scion David Koch.

Then, there was President Bill Clinton.

Clinton is never named in Epstein's little black book of contacts, although his close friend and counselor Doug Band is, along with a listing for "42." (Clinton was the forty-second president.)

In the flight logs for Epstein's Lolita Express, however, there was no such obfuscation. According to the logs, Clinton first hitchhiked on Epstein's infamous Lolita Express in February 2002. They were joined by Ghislaine, her "assistant" Sarah Kellen, four members of the Secret Service, and five people identified only as "male," "female," or by their initials.

According to the three-letter airport designations in the documents, the private jet flew from Miami International Airport to Westchester County Airport in New York State, where the Clintons have lived since 1999. On paper, it seems like an innocuous trip made by powerful men accustomed to brokering political and financial deals in unusual settings. But that notion changes when put into context.

President Clinton has claimed that he only traveled on Epstein's Lolita Express on four occasions.

Epstein and Clinton actually buddied up for six trips between 2002 and 2003, to Europe, Africa, and Asia. On their "humanitarian trips" to Africa, Clinton went without his usual security detail, and without chaperones. The men, it seemed, had hit it off.

"Jeffrey is both a highly successful financier and a committed philanthropist with a keen sense of global markets and an in-depth knowledge of 21st century science," Clinton said at the time, oozing his trademark characteristic sincerity. "I especially appreciated his insights and generosity during the recent trip to Africa to work on democratization, empowering the poor, citizen service, and combating HIV/AIDS."

Although Clinton referred to a single "trip" in his statement, in truth, they flew on Epstein's jet thirteen times during that eight-day overseas outing. What's more, they were routinely joined by controversial characters, like Hollywood actor—and accused pedophile—Kevin Spacey, who joined them on three of those flights, and Epstein's "personal massage therapist" Chauntae Davis, who got onboard in Cape Town and flew with them to Paris. Davis has since come forward with tales of Epstein's sexual abuse. (Spacey has denied all allegations of impropriety against him.)

"On almost every trip that I did go on, there were young girls around," Davis claimed.

In total, Clinton actually made twenty-seven trips with soon-to-be registered sex offender Epstein.

Clinton's press secretary would later insist that all of their flights were taken "in connection with the work of the Clinton Foundation" and that every leg included the applicable staff, foundation supporters and members of the secret service. Clinton denied that he ever knew of anything untoward happening on board.

At least one person, however, was suspicious. Cameron Humphries was director of the Santa Fe airport, just miles from the 10,000-acre Zorro Ranch, which Epstein purchased in 1993. He told reporter Katy Forrester, who collaborated on this book, that many people suspected how the Lolita Express had earned its name.

"When I was the manager there, it wasn't unusual to see large private aircraft flying. You know, Santa Fe is a destination, and a lot of people fly in with a private aircraft," Humphries said.

He continued:

What is unusual is to have somebody fly in with a large commercial type of aircraft that's been converted into their own private aircraft. I remember distinctly one afternoon there was a 737 that was sitting on a ramp. It was obviously a private aircraft and I was just curious, and so I asked one of the employees from the fixed base operator there.

A fixed base operator is a company that handles private aircraft instead of the commercial aircraft. They take care of the fueling and all of that. I asked one of the employees if they knew who owned it, and they had said "Jeffrey Epstein," and I had never heard the name before. This employee said, you know, "There's a rumor that he has a ranch here in New Mexico and that he flies in prostitutes. Some of them may not be of age of consent." Young girls was kind of the implication. He made it clear to me that it was a rumor, but I was really just appalled by this idea, if it were true.

I didn't know anything about him. I'd never heard the name before, so I didn't know if he'd been in prison or not or whatever, but I was so appalled by this idea that I called our airport law enforcement liaison officer and I said, "Hey listen, this is just a rumor, but there's this guy named Jeffrey Epstein that flew his private aircraft in, and apparently he's also flying in underage women to his ranch." I didn't know the guy, I'd never met him before, but you know, I was just so upset about this idea of this man flying around the country with that kind of impunity that I felt like I needed to tell somebody, so I reached out to our law enforcement officer.

He said that he had heard the rumors as well, and that it was his understanding that there was a federal investigation ongoing. That there was probably not much that they could do locally, but that he would certainly report it up. That was kind of the end of it for me, you know? After reporting it, knowing that that at least I had said something. I'll tell you, it was frustrating because it's a bit of a black hole, right? You report it, and then what?

The rumors were out there, so people knew it. And not only did people know it, there were people that were complicit in it. Why did it take so long?

Meanwhile, Epstein's escapades were also starting to raise eyebrows on the East Coast.

There, his team of drivers questioned why he had so many young girls as passengers.

Speaking here for the first time in print, Epstein's longtime chauffeur.

"I came forward in the hopes that I could help somebody, in the hopes that this doesn't happen to somebody else, in the hopes that these girls that are now seeking justice could find something," the chauffeur, who asked to remain anonymous, said. "My story may help, but I'm still afraid of what could happen."

From 2001 to 2011, this professional driver made more than five hundred runs for Epstein, his girls, and his associates.

"Back then, before 9/11, we used to actually pull up to the plane," the chauffeur recalled. "There were times when you'd have five cars outside of the plane and he would get in one and Ms. Maxwell and the girls would get in another, and then people I didn't recognize would get in other cars because it just seemed like he wanted to keep everybody separated."

The main port of call for Epstein's mile-high crime wave was Teterboro Airport. Located on the New Jersey side of the Hudson River, it is a thirty-minute drive to Epstein's uptown residence. The pimp and his posse used the transportation hub more than seven hundred times.

"I was astonished that somebody could fly around like that," he said. "He had a hectic schedule. He flew a $32 million jet like we drive our cars. . . . We had guys that were big time bankers, hedge fund managers and all that, that were customers of ours, celebrities that had jets. Nobody flew like he did. It was unbelievable."

Epstein certainly made an impression.

"Epstein was an arrogant, aggressive guy who was in total control of the situation," the chauffeur said. "He would sit back there and just direct you and give you orders. He was the king in the car. . . . I wasn't even in the car as far as he was concerned. He was more interested in the girls and joking and playing with them and pinching them on the cheek."

He continued:

> The girls seemed a little nervous and [Ghislaine] just kept reas-
> suring them, "Don't worry, everything will be okay. You'll be
> fine. Just do what I told you to do. And when it's all over you'll be
> very happy. You don't have to worry about anything and we'll get
> you home as soon as you're done."

They were young. They would fly in on his jet all the time. . . . I mean it's obvious. How could you have so many of these girls coming and going out of there? I mean, if we just dropped them off and left them there and picked them up in two weeks, you'd say, "Oh, well maybe it's his niece or whatever." But when you're dropping them off for two hours and driving them right back, something's up.

One time, he was with two girls. I assumed they were relatives or nieces. . . . But I didn't think anything of it at the time.

We picked him up at Newark Airport and we took him and these two young ladies. I guess they were about sixteen, seventeen years old. These girls today, they look older than they are. But we took him and these two girls to his apartment on Seventy-first Street.

Like I said, I thought it was his nieces or something or his daughters, because at that time nobody even had a clue what was going on. But as time went on, myself and other drivers assumed something was fishy because we kept picking up these teenage girls and he couldn't have that many nieces! We would some-times take them there to the apartment. And we were told to wait two, three hours and then drive back to the point.

So at that time we started getting suspicious and a lot of the drivers started saying, "You know what, I don't even want to drive for this guy anymore because there's something wrong." But needless to say, I needed the money at the time, I wasn't married that long. I was in the process of buying a house. I wasn't in a position to turn down rides. I didn't know what was going on.

So I continued the work, and looking back today when I see all this stuff that's come out, I feel terrible that maybe I could have done something to prevent people from being hurt at the time. When you look back, what are you going to do?

This was years before he was arrested. Nobody knew for sure, but we used to say, "Oh, I've got to go pick up the pedophile." And then all this comes out and it was true.

The chauffeur also was responsible for shuttling Epstein's pilot Dave Rodgers and his co-pilot Larry Visoski to their regular accommodations in the captain's building on Sixty-sixth Street.

"I drove them a lot," he admitted. "They never talked about where they went or who was on the plane. The only way I could gauge who was on the plane was the person that I was picking up. So they never talked about that kind of stuff. I guess, you know, he must have had them on a tight leash."

When Epstein was arrested in 2008, Rodgers and Visoski were grounded for more than a year. But Epstein found other ways of using them. According to the chauffeur, the pilots were ordered to drive the felon's Bentley from Florida to Texas to get it armor plated.

"Epstein was afraid that somebody was going to try to shoot him," the chauffeur claimed, recalling how the pilots "complained they had to drive all the way out there with the car because he was so paranoid."

"But they did it because they did whatever he was told to do. . . . You've got this guy that's overpowering them and giving them money. It's a sad state of affairs."

"We were like a courier service, so to speak," he said. "I overheard them talking one time that they had a safe there. Dave mentioned to Larry that Jeffrey called and wanted him to take the stuff that was out of the safe and bring it to him. So I don't know what it was, but there was a safe in that apartment."

Indeed, there was a safe—one that police cracked open after Epstein's second arrest, finding thousands of pictures and videos of unsuspecting subjects in sexual situations.

Looking in the proverbial rearview mirror, Epstein's personal chauffeur reflected on Epstein's gigantic web of blackmail, likening him to a mob boss.

"He was like the Godfather of the sky," the driver concluded. "He could do whatever he wanted, whenever he wanted, and nobody could touch him because he had money, he had influence, and he had dirt on all these people. And he was able to control and manipulate everything because everybody was afraid of him. Nobody would want that stuff to come out."

Today, the chauffeur has regrets about not coming forward sooner. Although, he and the other drivers certainly had their reasons.

"It just seems that these people with power and money and prestige, when they're involved in something, they will go out of their way and do anything they can to silence everybody."

"Epstein was paranoid years ago that someone was going to kill him and now he's dead," the driver explained. "They say it was suicide and whether it was or it wasn't. You know what? Karma's a bitch and you get what you've got coming. I think he was guilty of all that stuff and all the proof that's coming out says that it was true. So my feeling is that he got just what he deserved. It's just a shame that it happened so soon before these people could get their justice. But the bottom line is, he's gone and it's just another piece of garbage out of this world."

For the chauffeur, though, this tale has a particularly chilling ending.

"The guy who owned the company that I worked for, the Wednesday before Epstein killed himself, he died mysteriously in New Jersey," the chauffeur revealed. "I don't know if it's connected in any way, but it just seems funny that the guy who owned the company for all those years mysteriously died three days before he did."

"I don't know, it's crazy. But I don't want to end up like that."

More and more, it was becoming clear that Epstein was not just a jet-setting international playboy. Those around him, however, continued to keep their silence. Are they responsible for what followed?

Model and actress Alicia Arden told these authors that she was sexually assaulted by Epstein in 1997. Although she filed a police report, she claims, no one would listen to her allegations about the powerful businessman.

In May 1997, my good friend knew Jeffrey Epstein. She was in finance at the time, and I guess he was too, although no one seemed to know anything about him. I didn't even know who he was. I didn't hear of his name at all. So she apparently knew of him because she worked legitimately in finance. So she met him at the Beverly Hills Hotel.

She went in there in a different matter, of wanting to work with his company, or his company coming over to work with hers, or merging in some capacity. Some capacity in the finance world. And then he started telling her that she was really pretty, and "Do you want to model for Victoria's Secret?"

She was not a model, and she didn't want to do that. She said, "No, I don't want to model. But my friend Alicia does. You should meet her." So then Jeffrey said, "Have her call me. I work for Victoria's Secret. I could get her in the catalog." And she said, "Oh, great. She would love that." And then he told her, "Any other girls that you know of, have them call me." So then I did.

I called him and he told me to send my pictures to him, to his apartment on Madison Avenue, in New York. At the time, I was excited. I thought I was really going to get a picture or job in the Victoria's Secret catalog, because he told me that he worked for that. I was like, "This is great!" I was excited that I had kind of a hookup, where I'm not really going to go on an audition with a sea of girls.

I bought more Victoria's Secret lingerie, and I had a photographer shoot me in more pictures, in that specific brand, and then I sent those photos along with my existing book of pictures, my tear sheets.

I was not a model who was starting out. I had an array of work in tear sheets, and beautiful pictures. So I took all these extra pictures for him, along with the existing ones, and I Federal Expressed them to his apartment in Manhattan, on Madison.

He called me and said he got the pictures, and they were great, and he's going to have a woman named Kimberly, his secretary, call me to set up a time. So she did, and she said he was coming out there, to Santa Monica, California. And, "Would you like to meet him in the afternoon or the evening?"

It's not normal with all these modeling and acting jobs I've done, and auditions, for someone to call me and say we're going to meet in a hotel room. I have been in auditions in hotels, but there's other people, and you know that the casting is there. There's like a sign at the door, and you have to sign in, and you're there with a lot of other people. But I didn't think that there were going to be other people there that day. I thought, "This is a hookup. This is a major in, to getting in the Victoria's Secret catalog, because my friend met him and then the secretary's calling me, and he's already seen my pictures. So he likes me. I'm not going to have to go on a casting with other girls. He's just going to hire me, because he's already seen my pictures, and I'll get at least one picture in the catalog." So I was very happy about that.

I wanted to go in the afternoon. I thought that was better. I still had reservations about going into a hotel. But I thought, you know, this is Santa Monica, California, and this is Shutters. It's a very expensive, beautiful hotel. But I never went back, for anything, after I went there that day.

So it was set up in the afternoon. I was very excited. I mean I just visualized positive things, like, "I'm going to get in the Victoria's Secret catalog, and here's my portfolio, and just walk in and show my pictures to him, and then he can ask me about photos." Usually they ask you, "Where did you do that magazine? Did that come out? When was that? When did you take that picture?"

But I was just really expecting to already have the job, because of what had happened. My friend met him, the secretary called me, he said he worked for Victoria's Secret, and I thought, "Oh I'll get at least one picture. There's not a casting with all these other girls, or a sign-in sheet. It's just me meeting him, thinking like that picture would be great in the catalog."

Well, so I got there, and I walked in the front door, and he was kind of in the back, like in a kitchen, at a table. These hotels are kind of like, you could live there. It looks like a mini apartment. And they're on the beach.

He was kind of in the back, in a USA sweatshirt, and black sweatpants, and barefoot. Usually they are dressed a little bit more professional than that, the people who are auditioning.

I was sitting on the couch, kind of like I am now, and he was kind of far away from me. I went to give him my portfolio, and then I went back to the couch.

Then he was looking through it. I had a tendency sometimes to want to kind of stuff my bra a little bit to look bustier. I don't know why I was doing that, because nowadays they don't like you to do that in swimsuits and lingerie. But I did that, and then he was looking at my pictures, and then he was saying, "Oh, you look a little bustier in this picture, and you look a little bustier in that picture."

So I said, "Well, Jeffrey, I photograph different all the time. I'm very athletic. I could look bustier or not." Sometimes I would pad bras or wear two bras. I didn't really have to do that. I just kind of did it, and so he would make a comment on that.

Then he was looking and then he was saying, "Oh, well you look a little bit hippy in this picture." I said, "I mean I can photograph any way that you want. It's just the angle of the picture, the lighting, the photographer, or if I'm put in a skirt." So then he wanted me to come closer to him.

I got up off the couch, and then I walked closer to him, to the kitchen table. So he wanted me to come closer to him, and he said, "Well, let me see your hips and your butt." And he was just starting to look at me, and he said, "I need to manhandle you." So I came closer to him, and he was touching my chest, and my stomach, and then moved down to my hips and my butt.

He was kind of like evaluating my body, and then he started to lift up my skirt, kind of assisting me in undressing, and trying to take off my top. And I just thought, "You don't do this in a normal audition at all." So he was lifting up my skirt, and my top, and touching me, and he said, "I want to manhandle you." He said the word "manhandle" twice. And I've never heard that word from anyone ever again in my entire life. Not from anyone, like professional, nonprofessional, friends, or anything. I've never heard that word.

So he was touching my hips and my butt, and my buttocks and wanting to lift my skirt up and said he wanted to manhandle me. So I started to feel uncomfortable. And I just thought, "I have to get out of here before anything really bad happens." I had a friend who was raped and murdered around that time, so I always thought about that. I said to myself, "I never wanted to be raped. Never." I felt if I didn't leave, it could lead to that.

So, he was touching me. My shirt was kind of coming off. I just put it all down and got my book and went to leave. When I was doing that, he was putting a hundred dollars on the table.

I was like, "I don't need that, Jeffrey. I'm starting to feel like a prostitute. I don't need that. I'm not here for that." So I left it, and then I took my portfolio and I walked out of the hotel room.

I filed a police report. They weren't taking me seriously enough to even file. And then I went back a week later and did it anyway.

I guess the police officers ended up calling him, and he said, "Oh no. I don't know why she's doing that. She doesn't know what she's talking about." Meaning me. But I documented everything he said, in a report, and I've never done that in my entire life, before or after that. I never needed to do that, but I felt I needed to [do that], with him. And I documented everything. It's all in writing, saying that I went in there, and what happened.

If the police officers would've taken me seriously and kind of investigated him, all those years ago, then maybe . . . It's very upsetting, because I've thought about that for a long time. If the police officer and the Santa Monica Police Department would've investigated him, and taken me seriously, then I think he could have saved all the girls, the high school girls from being raped and attacked. Then maybe the girls could've been saved.

But I really wasn't taken seriously. My family, my friends discouraged me. Everyone discouraged me from going over there and filing the police report, because I wasn't physically raped.

I was assaulted, and I felt I could've been raped. He was touching me and taking my clothes off, and I felt if I didn't get out of there, it could've been worse. So did it need to be worse? Did I need to be raped? Did I physically need to be raped for anyone to take me seriously?

It could've saved all the girls from being attacked. And I don't know, his circle of friends, they just kind of put it under the cover, and socialized with him at events. That's what I saw in the news.

No one cared. Not just the police officers, but no one in his circle cared to see what he was doing.

For some of Epstein's friends, it was more that they *did* see what he was doing, but they just didn't care—because they were doing it, too.

What was it that brought these leaders of industry, media, and politics into the inner circle of a college dropout?

Maxwell family friend Laura Goldman has a theory, as she explains here:

I believe that Jeffrey Epstein was a genius, a savant, at understanding rich people.

This is what I know. Rich people are cheap, and rich people love nice things. What I believe that Jeffrey Epstein understood that and he provided people like Bill Gates, Bill Clinton with private planes, luxurious private planes and they just ate it up. It's a sad commentary on our society.

He understood that waving a private plane in front of Bill Clinton would make him a friend for life. He understood that offering a ride on the Lolita Express to Bill Gates and offering to talk to him about philanthropy would entice Bill Gates.

He understood your weak point. It may be that he was exceptionally good at it and exceptionally good at understanding rich people, but it is the method of all bullies to do that.

Epstein also paid for prestige, literally.

He gave $180,000 to the West Palm Beach nonprofit organization Ballet Florida and earmarked some of the cash for "therapeutic" massages. He gave $25,000 to a junior tennis center in Maryland, $30,000 to a preschool in New York, $15,000 to an all-girls private school a few blocks from his mansion in Manhattan, and, perhaps least unsurprisingly, nearly $100,000 to his former employer, Dalton.

From the 1990s through 2018, Epstein also gave hundreds of thousands of dollars to politicians on both sides of the aisle, including the Clintons and their foundation, President George H.W. Bush, Ohio Senator John Glenn, New York Senators Charles Schumer and Daniel Patrick Moynihan, Senate Majority Leader Bob Dole, Ohio Governor John Kasich, former Secretary of State John Kerry, and New Mexico Governor Bill Richardson (who would later be named in court documents as a coconspirator, a claim he vehemently denies).

This is not a case of guilt by association. All of those men insist they had no idea what Epstein was doing. But ultimately, there *were* people who knew what was going on and could have had stopped Epstein's exploitation . . . and no one did.

"They either indulge in these behaviors, or they like that someone does," Goldman said of the uber-rich. "Why hasn't been Bill Gates been forced to answer why he was on the Lolita Express? Why is Leslie Wexner still CEO of The Limited? Anyone that allegedly facilitated Jeffrey Epstein's crimes should serve a minimum of twenty years in jail. I do not think those people are redeemable. There's no way to rehabilitate them."

Epstein's former friend Kornbluth, meanwhile, suggests that powerful men are conditioned to believe that presumption of guilt "does not apply" to them.

> No one says "no" to them. No one. The idea that these men would have sex with an underage girl, and that that would cause them any trouble, any blowback, it doesn't occur."

Worst of all, Goldman said, are the British aristocracy.

"I think that the French and the English and the aristocracy of Europe are deviants," she told Marc Lupo.

At least one is.

CHAPTER 6
RANDY ANDY

Jeffrey Epstein and Ghislaine Maxwell were playing a dangerous game, cultivating famous friends in the name of an international blackmail and intelligence scheme. The Duke of York—also known as Prince Andrew, eighth in line to the British throne—was their ultimate trophy.

According to Maxwell family friend Laura Goldman, Epstein came into Prince Andrew's life because Ghislaine Maxwell "became friendly" with his scandal-scarred ex-wife Sarah Ferguson, Duchess of York.

"Fergie introduced Ghislaine to Prince Andrew and then Ghislaine introduced Prince Andrew to Jeffrey Epstein," she said.

Prince Andrew had divorced Sarah "Fergie" Ferguson in 1996, and was living it up as one of the world's most eligible bachelors. Fergie was front-page tabloid fodder herself, photographed having her toes sucked by a Texan millionaire in what was the royal family's biggest scandal ever—at least, at the time.

Fergie stayed in touch with Epstein well after the divorce. In 2005, she left a phone message for Epstein at his Palm Beach home, obtained by this team, that notes she was "expecting" his call. In 2014, she admitted she'd taken cash from Epstein to help settle her postdivorce debt.

Meanwhile, Andrew was working as a British trade envoy, tasked with using his position to promote British business and drive investment around the world. It was a role he relished, because it also catered to the fast-paced lifestyle to which he had always been accustomed. He even earned the nickname "Air Miles Andy" because of his jet-setting. As he traveled the world, little did he know, he would soon overtake his ex as the most scandalous royal ever.

Andy also earned another nickname because of his bad boy behavior: "Randy Andy, or "Handy Andy." In Epstein, the raucous royal found a kindred spirit.

Their bond became so tight, Epstein and Ghislaine were invited as guests of honor to a June 2000 party at Windsor Castle, the Queen's weekend home.

Called "Dance of the Decades," the party was the most exclusive royal event in years, celebrating the birthdays of Andrew, who was turning forty, Prince Charles, who was fifty, Princess Margaret's seventieth, and Prince William's eighteenth. Obviously, the Queen and Prince Phillip were on hand to celebrate.

A few months later, Andrew was again partying with Epstein, this time at Heidi Klum's Halloween party in New York, with Ghislaine as his date. The costume she chose for accompanying one of Britain's highest royals? A prostitute.

In December, Andrew and Epstein returned to England for a weekend at the royal Sandringham estate—the Queen's country home. After Christmas, the pair was then photographed together in Phuket, Thailand, relaxing on a luxury yacht and surrounded by topless girls. Queen Elizabeth was not amused.

Still, the scandal didn't end Epstein and Andrew's friendship.

A few months later, Andrew made the long trip out to Epstein's New Mexico Zorro Ranch. Deidre Stratton personally waited on his every need during that visit, and spoke publicly for the first time to reporter Katy Forrester, one of the collaborators on this book.

I had to serve him. I'm guessing 2001. Three days, maybe.

There were pictures of him with Ghislaine and him and Jeffrey in the house. I had been told that Jeffrey and Andrew went way back.

You know, at that time he was very, very pleasant. You could understand his lifestyle. We put him in a three bedroom, it's called the Lodge. It's really very nice and the setting of it was gorgeous. There was this beautiful deck that overlooked this great kind of valley that was really stunning, and it was nice enough that they sat outside. So that would indicate late summer, early fall.

But that's where he stayed and his bodyguard stayed down at what we called Ranch Central. For him to just be out on his own, I'm sure was very different for him.

And of course, we all felt like, "What do we do? We're like fish out of water. Do we curtsy to this man?" And we were told no, because we're not British subjects. So we didn't have to show any particular, you know, whatever to him.

He wasn't married at the time, and I thought he was very gracious. He was so gracious. He didn't act appalled at all that here he was put up in this remote manufactured home out in the sticks and given someone like me to serve him. Which, I'm no footman. I guarantee that. And so I just thought he kind of thought it was novel.

I offered to come up there and fix his breakfast. So he goes, "No, I want to try." So when I got up there later to tidy up, you could smell burnt bacon. And he's like, "I didn't do so well."

He had a croissant with cream cheese or something. But I remember him trying to cook his own breakfast. Isn't that cute? And he couldn't even fry bacon.

I do recall one other thing. I had to serve him some kind of food and I used garlic in it. Later, he told me that as a child he ate a whole bulb of garlic, and since that time garlic just turns him nauseated. I do recall that, and he was very good natured about that. I bet he was hungry, but he was good-natured.

I don't know what he did. I don't recall him being very sporty.

Still, Andrew found other means of entertainment.

"At the time, Jeffrey had this, supposedly she was a neurosurgeon, quite young. Not young, young, young, but beautiful, young and brilliant," Stratton remembered.

"She stayed in the home with Andrew and at one point we had all these different teas that you could pick the tea that you wanted. She asked me to find one that would make him more horny, that he hadn't been interested in her. I'm guessing because she understood her job was to entertain him.

"Jeffrey probably had her on retainer and she knew what her job would be. Should be, you know, to make these people happy. That's what I thought. I do recall them sharing at least one dinner."   .

Why would Epstein have invited a British royal out to the middle of nowhere, and set him up with a strange woman?

Stratton supposed, "I have read where the island was set up with cameras where Jeffrey could tape these men with their underage people and use it as blackmail. I mean that's the oldest game in the book, isn't it?"

***

Around the same time, a few months before or after Prince Andrew's New Mexico stay, Ghislaine and Epstein flew to London to meet up with their favorite British party pal. Along for the ride, according to allegations, was seventeen-year-old Virginia Roberts.

"That first time in London I was so young," Roberts would later tell a reporter for the *National Enquirer*. "Ghislaine woke me up in the morning and said, 'You're going to meet a prince today.' I didn't know at that point that I was going to be trafficked to that prince."

According to Roberts, Ghislaine stated something to the effect of, "He's coming back to the house and I want you to do for him what you do for Epstein." Later, Roberts would claim that she had been Epstein's personal sex slave for months at the time.

Roberts alleged the encounter with Prince Andrew took place at Ghislaine's London home.

A photo taken at the same location would later emerge, showing Prince Andrew with his arm around Virginia's bare midriff, and a grinning Ghislaine in the background.

Roberts continued:

> She asked Andrew how old he thought I was. He guessed 17. They all kind of laughed about it, and Ghislaine made a joke that I was getting "too old" for Jeffrey.
>
> He was groping me. He touched my breasts. He touched my ass. He was not my type, but I'd been trained not only to not show my emotions, but to do what [was] wanted.
>
> He started licking my toes, between my toes, the arches of my feet.
>
> He proceeded to make love to me. . . . He wasn't rude. It wasn't like rape, but it wasn't like love, either. It was more like, "I'm getting my business done."

Andrew didn't use a condom during their encounter, she claimed: "Jeffrey knew I was on the pill."

To wrap up the night, Roberts alleged that she and Andrew took a bath together, and that Epstein paid her $10,000 the following day.

There was more horror to come.

According to Roberts, there was another, equally terrifying encounter, one that began with the prince arriving "smiling ear-to-ear."

> He looked like a kid whose parents were taking him to Disney World. I took him upstairs to the "dungeon."
>
> He was fondling me and we undressed and he lay on the table facedown. I did my normal routine, which was to start with the feet, up the calves, tickling the thighs, up the buttocks, up the back. On this occasion I don't think I made it up to his shins when he flipped over.

I was just another person he was bedding. He couldn't have cared less about me as a young woman. . . . He was being treated to sex for which someone else was paying.

From the snickering noises he was making, he was really enjoying the whole thing, but I felt like a total prostitute. He never even said, 'Did you enjoy it?' I was there for just one purpose.

Another young girl under Epstein's control, Johanna Sjoberg, claimed to have been present during that encounter as well, and recounted a grotesque scene: Prince Andrew using a puppet of himself to grope the young girls' breasts.

"He thought it was funny because it was him," Sjoberg stated in a 2016 deposition, obtained in our investigation.

During another trip, at Epstein's private island, Roberts's description of a third encounter with Prince Andrew was even more debauched.

She claimed:

A group of Russian girls who didn't speak a word of English turned up with a modeling agent who was a friend of Jeffrey's. That night there was a dinner and Andrew was there. He said 'hi' to me.

Jeffrey directed us with hand gestures because the Russian girls didn't speak English. We were told to start kissing and touching and to use sex toys on each other. The girls obviously had been trained. Jeffrey and the prince were laughing . . . and then they undressed and then I performed a sex act on them—Jeffrey first and then Andrew. It was disgusting. There was no pleasure in it.

Prince Andrew left the following night.

Buckingham Palace strongly disputes Roberts's claims, as does Prince Andrew. In 2015, a judge ordered them to be struck from the court record in a legal case that she had filed.

"I just wish to reiterate and to reaffirm the statements which have already been made on my behalf by Buckingham Palace," the prince stated at the time, denying her allegations. "My focus is on my work."

However, certified voice stress expert Michael Sylvestre, who analyzed audio of Andrew's statement, concluded the prince showed "extreme" tension while making the statement.

"He's lying. Andrew knows the statement made by Buckingham Palace was not true," Sylvestre claimed.

Sylvestre ran the clip through the DecepTech Voice Stress Analysis Machine, a computerized version of the Psychological Stress Evaluation, which is used by more than fifty law enforcement agencies in the United States. The test is said to be superior to a conventional polygraph. The machine senses stress levels in the voice; frequent "peaks" on the readout indicate that the speaker is being dishonest.

The DecepTech Voice Stress Analysis Machine prints out elevated lines on a chart when it detects deception. The readout of Andrew's evaluation, Sylvester says, is clear: "The deception started pretty much from the beginning. The chart shows he was definitely not reiterating or reaffirming what was said by the palace."

Sharing the same conclusion is body language and speech expert Susan Constantine, who noted that Andrew failed to mention what he was "reiterating or reaffirming"—a sign that he's trying to deceive.

"A deceptive person naturally leaves out incriminating information and won't speak of it or put himself into the event. He also refused to describe the sexual allegations," she said.

"Historically, with people who are trying to be deceptive, especially when it comes to sexual offenses, they won't name the crime.

"A truthful person would say, 'I did not have sex with the person,' because they know they are innocent."

It wouldn't be the last statement of denial that Prince Andrew would make in regard to Epstein.

CHAPTER 7

DIARY OF A SEX SLAVE

Prince Andrew wasn't the only associate of Jeffrey Epstein to cruelly take advantage of one of the financier's teens. By this time, Epstein had developed an entire roster of young, vulnerable, women that he pimped out to his powerful contacts as a means of gaining influence and leverage.

One of these sex slaves was Virginia Roberts.

Like many of the girls targeted by Epstein, Roberts had experienced a rough childhood: When she was twelve, a close family friend sexually abused her. She developed an eating disorder and ran away from home and started living on the streets at age thirteen.

Virginia told the story of her dark early years in a secret handwritten diary obtained by this investigation.

"I was on the streets," Roberts began.

There, she wrote: "I was picked up by a 67-year-old man who did exactly what Jeffrey did with me, abuse and violate my youthfulness."

That man—a far cry from the hero he initially seemed to be—was Ron Eppinger, boss of the modeling agency Perfect 10. His business was actually a front for international sex trafficking, and he soon made Roberts his personal "employee."

Roberts claimed Eppinger got her hooked on opioids, the highly addictive class of drugs that include heroin, synthetic opioids such as fentanyl, and pain relievers such as oxycodone, Vicodin, codeine, and morphine. Under his drug-fueled spell, according to Roberts, Eppinger committed "outrageous acts of hedonism."

Shortly after her fourteenth birthday, Roberts described, Eppinger "gifted" her to a wealthy client named Charlie, who continued the abuse and degradation.

The FBI eventually raided his home, and Roberts's father arrived to save her. Eppinger later pleaded guilty to charges of alien smuggling for prostitution, interstate travel for prostitution, and money laundering.

Reeling from the nightmare, Roberts checked into the Growing Together substance abuse treatment facility in Lake Worth, Florida.

There, the horror continued. Growing Together was "the most controversial drug-treatment program in Palm Beach County," Florida's *Sun Sentinel* newspaper wrote in a 1990 investigative report. Former patients claimed they experienced "torture" and "brainwashing," and left with "PTSD like a Vietnam War veteran." A later *New York Times* investigation found "physical and sexual abuse appears to be common there."

"I still can't get the screams out of my head from hearing kids dragged down the hall by the hair on their heads," a former graduate of the program told the *Broward Palm Beach New Times* in 2004. "The crimes that were committed there have never been told in public. Nobody has ever put these people on trial."

"Could things like this happen in an institutional setting? Yes," Growing Together Executive Director Pat Allard told the paper, while denying the charges. "Would it blemish the institution? Yes, it would. Would anyone condone it? Absolutely not."

The facility later closed.

Roberts wrote that she was locked in a "white room" during her stay and that fights with orderlies were a regular occurrence.

With the help of her father and brother, though, she managed to escape. Roberts slowly got back on track and decided to pursue a career in massage therapy. In the summer of 1998, she landed a job in the spa at the newly anointed Mar-a-Lago Club—owned by Donald Trump. She was optimistic about the future.

While studying at work one day, Roberts was approached by a "striking beautiful woman" who lived a mile down the street. It was Ghislaine, and she offered the fifteen-year-old a job with "a very wealthy gentleman who was always on the lookout for a new masseuse."

"I agreed," Roberts remembered, confessing that it sounded like "the legit break I had been wanting."

The excited young girl told her father about the encounter. Admittedly, he was skeptical, and a little confused.

"I thought it was a job where she was just going to learn massage therapy," he later said. "That is what she told me. I did not know it was going to be all this other stuff."

To make sure everything was kosher, Roberts personally brought his daughter over to Epstein's mansion for the first visit. He discussed the situation with Ghislaine, who introduced him to Epstein.

"He came across as a nice guy," her father would claim. "I had no idea what he would end up doing. If I had known differently, I would never have let her work there."

Satisfied, the hoodwinked father left Roberts in the hands of the sex predators. Wasting no time, Ghislaine brought the aspiring masseuse to Epstein's master bathroom.

"Bedazzled by the décor, I shook out of my entranced state and tried not to gawk at the naked man that lay atop a massage table," Roberts wrote. "I acted calm and cool. [Ghislaine] introduced Jeffrey Epstein as a multi-billion-dollar banker and stock broker that took delight in a massage at least once a day."

Ghislaine then showed her the ropes, starting at the toes and working her way up Epstein's body.

"They really had me convinced they were smart, intellectual people wanting to help me learn a trade," Roberts explained.

Everything changed, however, when Epstein rolled over. First, Ghislaine took her own top off and briefly pressed her chest against Epstein, Roberts alleged. Next, Ghislaine started undressing the teen, who was too stunned to resist.

"I was asked to indulge Jeffrey in oral sex while Ghislaine caressed me from behind, cupping my small breasts and feeling me inside," Roberts later described in one of her secret diaries.

"I was inclined to scream out of humiliation for being so damned naïve." She added:

> Jeffrey moaned out of delight and pulled up my chin to look at me then guided my hips to sit on top of him. He next forcibly entered me and used his hips to gratify his sexual needs. As soon as it was over, I quickly got dressed, and not sure how to keep my composure, just kept quiet. They both thanked me for a job well done as I had passed my trial.

Epstein paid Virginia $200 for her two-hour session and had an employee drive her home.

"I was now a hired prostitute," she later described.

Stuck in a "state of shock," the embarrassed teenager didn't dare tell her father. Her previous confession about the family friend, and her subsequent time with a sex trafficker, had torn her family apart. She had finally rebounded into something "normal." So when the offer to return to the mansion came in, Epstein and Ghislaine seemed, at the time, the lesser of two evils.

For Roberts, escaping a life as the personal sex slave of the rich and powerful seemed inescapable.

Over the next few weeks, the pair thoroughly abused Roberts under the pretext of "domestic sex slave" training, she wrote.

"It was everything down to how to give a blowjob, how to be quiet, be subservient, give Jeffrey what he wants," she claimed. "A lot of this training came from Ghislaine herself . . . and then there's Jeffrey who's telling you, 'I want it this way, go slower.'"

(Ghislaine has strongly denied Roberts's allegations, but she certainly did train staffers in some ways. This team obtained a phone message from inside Epstein's home that recorded a call from Ghislaine. Epstein's assistant wrote that the message was "would be helpful to have [redacted] come to Palm Beach today to stay here and help train new staff with Ghislaine.")

As for Epstein, however, Roberts was hardly the first victim. She was, though, perhaps the pedophile's pet project, and soon she became their most socially valuable asset.

According to Roberts's recollections, the trio moved between Epstein's New York and Palm Beach mansions, where she was given her own luxurious rooms at each property. Their daily activities began to include the use of sex toys, Roberts claimed, which were kept piled in a laundry basket. Roberts said she also was initiated into sadism and masochism, otherwise known as S&M, the practice of taking or causing abuse during sex.

"It was basically every day and was like going to school," she wrote in the diaries.

"You just become this numb figure who refuses to feel and refuses to speak. All you do is obey."

Roberts was under the impression that her masters eventually planned to hook her up with one of their rich and powerful friends so she would be "set up for life." She had no clue that she would be pimped out as the sexual plaything to many individuals in Epstein and Maxwell's social circle.

Shortly before Roberts's sixteenth birthday, she wrote in the diaries, Epstein and Ghislaine broke the news.

"They wanted me to be able to cater to all the needs of the men they were going to send me to," Roberts claimed. "They wanted me to produce things for them in addition to performing sex on men. They told me to pay attention to the details about what the men wanted, so I could report back to them."

When Roberts looked openly confused, Epstein explained to the child that he wanted to "have something on them." More than just a sex slave, he was now making Roberts a cog in his personal spy wheel.

"Epstein specifically told me that the reason for him doing this was so that they would 'owe him;' they would 'be in his pocket,'" Roberts alleged.

She supposed, "Epstein thought he could get leniency if he was ever caught doing anything illegal, or more so that he could escape trouble altogether."

To get her started, Epstein and Ghislaine sent Roberts to Little St. James with "a professor" and told her to take care of him as she had Epstein, she wrote in the diary. After receiving a favorable report from the john, the diabolical pair then continued sending Roberts into the dens of predators around the world. She started making $400 an hour working for Epstein, she wrote, and moved in with him full-time.

"I mean, in some ways, we were a little fucked up family," Virginia later told the *Miami Herald*. "It was, 'Jeffrey needs to have sex at least seven times a day . . . but in the meantime, we're gonna sit back and have some popcorn while you're giving a blowjob and watching *Sex and the City*. It was just a really screwed up kind of little family unit."

Epstein and Ghislaine took her on wild shopping sprees, had her meals prepared by a personal chef, and even celebrated her sweet sixteen on the orgy island.

They also offered to double her salary for recruiting more girls, she alleged.

"Jeffrey would send me out to go talk to pretty girls, the younger the better," Roberts wrote. "I would offer them money to come meet my gentlemen friend and tell them I'd show them how to massage. . . . I never brought back a girl that ever said no, or didn't want to participate in an erotic massage for money."

Roberts's diary corroborates the fact that documenting the underage exploits of the rich and powerful was a major component of Epstein's master plan. He had installed security cameras in every room of his properties, and throughout his Caribbean island. Epstein also employed full-time AV techs to monitor dozens of video feeds.

"Kill two birds with one stone Jeffrey thought," Roberts wrote. "Free porn to share with his pedophile friends and when the occasion called for it, a security system all at one expense."

Meanwhile, Epstein continued to maximize his assets by sending his Boeing 727 into overdrive.

"It's called Lolita Express for a reason," Roberts wrote. "That was a vessel for him to be able to abuse girls and get away with it."

Among the men who she claims violated her in Epstein's mile-high club were *The Simpsons* creator Matt Groening (who gave her a personally inscribed sketch of Homer and Bart); model scout Jean-Luc Brunel (another reported sex trafficker who could secure passports for minors); cofounder of MIT's artificial intelligence lab, Marvin Minsky; and former US Senate Majority Leader George Mitchell. ("I have never met, spoken with or had . any contact with Ms. Giuffre," the Maine senator has denied. At the time of this writing, Groening has not issued a public denial. Brunel is missing. Minsky is dead.)

As for Epstein's friend Donald Trump, Roberts wrote that he was a not-unfrequent presence in their twisted world, but she never saw him indulge: "I didn't physically see him have sex with any of the girls. . . . I can't say who he had sex with in his whole life or not, but I just know it wasn't with me when I was with other girls." In a later court deposition she even denied that he'd ever flirted with her.

By late 2001, Ghislaine began shuttling Roberts around in a private-ly-owned helicopter. Even more discreet than the Lolita Express, the heli-copter created still more opportunities for abuse.

In court documents unsealed in July 2019, Roberts alleged that she was forced to give "massages" to then-twenty-five-year-old filmmaker and envi-ronmentalist Alexandra Cousteau, the granddaughter of famous French explorer Jacques Cousteau.

Roberts said that Epstein "instigated that she and I reenact as lovers in lesbian acts of foreplay and penetration" with a strap-on penis.

"The allegations by Virginia Giuffre née Roberts regarding Ms. Cousteau are 100 percent false," Cousteau's lawyer wrote in an email statement soon after the court files were released. "Ms. Cousteau never had intimate rela-tions with Giuffre, and does not even recall ever having met such a person."

(Cousteau does have, however, links to one of Epstein's closest business partners: Saudi Arabian Crown Prince Mohammed bin Salman. Epstein had a framed photo of "MBS" in his Manhattan mansion and often claimed the controversial Saudi royal had visited his property there many times, these authors can reveal. In 2019, it was reported that MBS ordered the assassination of journalist Jamal Khashoggi, nephew of Epstein's infamous pal Adnan Khashoggi. In September 2019, Cousteau was named as one of the featured speakers at a conference sponsored by the United Nations and a foundation headed by MBS.)

Meanwhile, shortly before Roberts's eighteenth birthday, it was time for her to meet Prince Andrew.

As Roberts tells it, it was the darkest time of her life. The young girl had been inhumanely used and abused, and had even suffered a miscarriage. She hadn't known she was pregnant, she wrote, or who the dead baby's father was. Epstein had promised to cut back her hours if she brought in more girls, she claimed, but the fresh faces only dragged the weary working girl into more threesomes.

Roberts would soon age out of Epstein's preferred bracket—women fourteen to seventeen. According to Roberts, though, they still could make use of her.

"Ghislaine starts talking to me about how I would feel about having a child," Virginia recently alleged, claiming that she was offered $200,000 a month and a house in exchange for the baby.

The idea terrified her. After years of being emotionally, physically, and mentally degraded, Roberts had reached rock bottom. She began plotting her escape.

Roberts managed to convince Epstein and Ghislaine to send her to Thailand in search of legitimate massage training. Epstein agreed under one condition: that she bring back "a Thai girl."

In the summer of 2002, Roberts fled to Thailand, where she met and fell in love with martial artist Robert Giuffre. Newly empowered and determined to begin her own life on the other side of the world, the girl made one final call to her captors, Ghislaine and Epstein.

"He said, 'Have a nice life,' and hung up," Virginia said of her brief goodbye phone call with Epstein. "I thought, 'I'm off the hook, I'm off the chain, I can go, I can live free.'"

Roberts and her new man eloped, moved to Australia, and started a family.

Still, despite her wish for freedom, the nightmare wasn't over.

In 2007, while pregnant with her second child, Virginia claimed she received a call from Ghislaine.

"I was like, 'How the hell did she just find me?'" Roberts wondered. "'I've been out of their lives for so long.'"

According to Roberts, by then going by the name Virginia Giuffre, Ghislaine wanted to know if she had "talked to anybody." The former sex slave informed her that she hadn't, she claimed. Seemingly satisfied with her answer, Ghislaine ordered her to "stay quiet."

"The next day Jeffrey calls me, with his lawyer on the phone, and he asks me the same questions," Giuffre recently alleged.

Concerned, the new mother wondered what was going on. The next day, the FBI called and asked about her sexual history with Epstein. She demanded the officer verify his employment.

"About six months later, I get a knock at the door and it's the Australian Federal Police," she said. (The Australian Federal Police is like the FBI, the national and principal federal law enforcement agency.)

Officials gave her a detailed document about what Jeffrey had done, and how she'd been identified as a victim: "Jane Doe #3."

Remarkably, more than nine thousand miles from Epstein and Ghislaine, she was still so frightened by the long-arm of the lawless pedophile, she refused to assist the officers.

Little did she know that a massive investigation was unfolding across the world in her home state of Florida—one that could finally bring Epstein to justice.

CHAPTER 8

DONALD TRUMP AND
THE PALM BEACH PEDOPHILE

Palm Beach in the late eighties and nineties was the perfect playground for a man like Jeffrey Epstein: decadent, debaucherous, and deeply corrupted.

"I spent a lot of time in Palm Beach at that time," said Maxwell family friend Laura Goldman.

She continued:

> Palm Beach is a live-and-let-live kind of place. Lots of rich libertarian types. I don't think that they mixed with their neighbors, because they didn't want their neighbors to know what they were doing. I think the police force down there is pretty ineffective. We've seen that they are. I think that people are there on vacation, they didn't want to rock the boat.
>
> I spent a lot of time in Palm Beach at that time. I'd been to their house on Brillo Way. It was kind of not my scene and there were lots of young ladies. Even though I was much younger then, they were even younger than me, and I really couldn't compete in that scene.
>
> Now I feel bad because I got a sense that something was off. I didn't really pay attention to what was off. Now, when I see what's happened to all these girls, I feel incredibly terrible that I didn't ride by more often, like a bike crusader, and stop it.

Everybody knew that he was looking for young girls. But I didn't realize, one, that they were young, that young, and I didn't realize that he was trafficking them. But it doesn't surprise me that the Palm Beach police looked away.

People don't understand about Palm Beach in the nineties and at that time, there was no South Beach. So, Palm Beach was where all the decadent people went. The Palm Beach police kind of looked the other way.

I visited with other people Jeffrey Epstein's house in the late nineties. I noticed that it wasn't the grandest house on the block, but it was the most private.

Another visitor, Epstein's former attorney Alan Dershowitz, told this investigation's reporter, Jen Heger, that the home held many secrets.

Insisting he knew nothing of Epstein's illegal escapades, Dershowitz described, "In his house in Palm Beach, there were two stairways. One of them, you were not allowed to go up."

"He had locked doors," Dershowitz continued. "I was never in that part of the house. The same thing is true in his house in New York."

Those doors were finally opened, however, during a later police raid on the home. After years of relentlessly hounding the local authorities, these authors were able to obtain the official video. The following is a description of its content:

Many guests entered the home through the kitchen, a bright and airy space with a black and white checkered floor and cozy bar stools around the island. Heading through there to a back staircase, however, it got literally darker.

Carpeted in lilac and bound by white walls, the staircase spiraled up to the upper level, home to several bedrooms, bathrooms, and of course, the massage room.

It all begins innocently enough. At the top of the staircase is a landing with pink carpeting and a comfy pink couch. There's a photograph of palm trees and the ocean.

Turning left, you enter a den of several tiny bedrooms—rooms scarcely big enough to hold both a bed and a dresser, but bright and bedecked with cheap art. In nearly every room, the only item of clothing to see was a white robe. In another bedroom, there was a teddy bear.

Moving back across the landing and to the right, the atmosphere changes. First, there is an antechamber of sorts, a dark room with chairs, similar to a waiting area. On the wall, a close-up photo shows hands tightly gripping someone's leg, fingers digging into the flesh. On another wall hung a photo so graphic it was the only image blurred from the police video. [Attorney Spencer Kuvin would later tell our team that one of his clients, a victim of Epstein, remembered one photo "of a young girl who could have been no more than twelve or thirteen years old with her panties pulled down around her ankles bent over."] Dominating another wall was a 3-D rendering of a woman's torso, seen from the back, and cut off just below and above the rear end. The curves protrude inches from the wall.

Moving deeper into the next room, that same rear view is re-created in a painting. Another painting shows a nude woman lying down with her legs spread, dark pubic hair at the center of the frame; her breasts, very small.

Moving deeper still: the massage room. Immediately upon entry, there is a large ink drawing of Ghislaine smiling softly and looking toward the massage table, as if she presides over what would happen there. Below her, a small model airplane calls to mind the Lolita Express. At the back of the room, the massage table.

There are oils, lotions, and a large vibrating "massager" (later described by multiple victims as an instrument of sexual assault). More stacked towels, more hanging robes. His bedroom is nearby.

In Epstein's personal quarters, the "art" becomes even more disturbing. One photograph captures a wet woman in the shower, from behind. A line drawing depicts a naked woman's torso from the side. Yet another, directly from the front. Yet another, a naked woman curled in the fetal position. Not far away, stacks of personal stationery bearing his name.

In a closet filled with men's clothes, dozens of small, personal photographs are framed, collage-style on the walls. Most show young women. Most of them are topless. There's also a picture of Epstein and a brunette standing in front of the United States Presidential Seal, in what appears to be the White House briefing room.

Still more candid photos of female companions bedeck the walls of his personal gym, downstairs and off the pool. One image shows a blonde toddler, missing teeth, grinning into the camera as she climbs out of a pool. Another, a blonde toddler in a dress. Still another, a young blonde girl with no pubic hair stretched out naked and apparently unconscious on a beach. An extremely tight closeup of a female rear end.

Tucked away in the gym bathroom, there is a photo of an arrogant-looking man—not Epstein. Featured in our photo insert, the man has an amber, almost orange hair sculpted into a perilous combover. His hand, rather small, is raised casually in the air as his elbow rests on the arm of his chair. He wears a billowy, ill-fitting button-down and slacks, staring pompously, with his lips pursed, into the camera. Behind him, a young brunette in a white tank top stands with her hands just above his shoulders, as if she was in the midst of giving him a massage. Behind her, another young brunette returns the favor, massaging the first girl's shoulders as well. Behind the second brunette, a blonde in the chunky black sandals popular with nineties teens grins at the camera while massaging the second girl. A four-way massage, as only Epstein could orchestrate.

Donald Trump and Jeffrey Epstein were close friends during that heady Palm Beach era.

"I've known Jeff for 15 years," Trump told *New York* magazine in 2002, placing his first connection with Epstein in 1987, two years *before* he would step foot on Robert Maxwell's *Lady Ghislaine* yacht.

"He's a terrific guy," Trump continued. "It is even said that he likes beautiful women as much as I do, and many of them are on the younger side." If he believed that, why didn't he report Epstein to the police? Perhaps he didn't think the girls were that young. Or perhaps it was because he was, in some form, Epstein's wingman.

In the early nineties, following Trump's divorce from Ivanka Trump, the two were constant companions.

A recently unearthed archival video from 1992, recorded by NBC News, shows the two pervy playboys whispering and laughing, surrounded by women at Trump's Mar-a-Lago—the same place from which Virginia Roberts had been recruited. Next to them was an editor for the *National Enquirer*, Larry Haley, who was reported to have been assigned full-time to the Trump "beat" for the scandal sheet.

In 2000, Trump and Epstein were photographed attending an event on the same property with Prince Andrew and Trump's wife Melania.

According to insiders, Trump had full privileges at Epstein's Palm Beach home, as well. He's since denied ever being close with Epstein, but attorney Spencer Kuvin, who represents one of Epstein's victims, claims the evidence suggests otherwise.

"We knew from deposition testimony that we took in the civil cases from a few of the people that work within Mr. Epstein's home that Donald Trump was more than just a casual acquaintance of Mr. Epstein," he told reporter Doug Montero.

> We knew that because even on one occasion, we were aware that Mr. Trump had come to the house and stopped by and just ate in Mr. Epstein's kitchen. And just sat there, and chatted, and ate in the kitchen with him. So, this was more than just a casual acquaintance. This was somebody that he knew and that they spoke with one another, they socialize with one another.
>
> We also knew that Epstein and Trump had gone to parties together at Mar-a-Lago that Mr. Trump had arranged. We knew that one of the victims that came forward and accused Epstein of

essentially turning her into a sex slave was found at Mar-a-Lago originally, she was working there, and that's where Epstein got her from.

So, we also know through stories that have come forward now from two young girls that were sisters that were in the New York area, that Mr. Trump had stopped by Mr. Epstein's New York home on occasion as well. So as far as high-profile friends, we certainly knew that Mr. Trump was a close friend of Mr. Epstein during those exact years that Mr. Epstein was molesting these young girls. . . . These are two gentlemen that definitely ran in the same circles.

Later, Epstein's flight logs would show an entry for Trump on the Lolita Express. Not only was his phone number found in Epstein's little black book; but also, more than a dozen additional ways to contact him.

After Epstein's crimes became public, Trump attempted to distance himself. He reportedly barred Epstein from Mar-a-Lago in 2008, and said in 2019, "I knew him like everybody in Palm Beach knew him," insisting, "I was not a fan."

Indeed, during those years Epstein was an inescapable and infamous figure in Palm Beach, one who made little effort to conceal his dark deeds from friends, acquaintances, and even strangers. Although few were invited upstairs or into his more personal quarters, his home was small, and the images could easily have been discovered.

As Epstein threw raucous parties for Palm Beach's elite, was he toeing the line, taking some small thrill from the possibility of being exposed? Or was he using the sexual images and young women throughout the property as bait?

Kuvin told Montero: "We had heard that Mr. Epstein had created videos of high-profile individuals inside of his home and kept them as insurance. And maybe he had provided women to some of these individuals, or young girls."

Maxwell family friend Laura Goldman attended one such debaucherous party at the Palm Beach mansion, and was disturbed by what she found.

"There was a bar in Palm Beach in the nineties called Chuck & Harold's," Goldman explained. "It's not there anymore. Somebody there invited me to the party. Most of the crowd at that place at the bar scene were old Palm Beach, Wall Streeters and that kind of people."

She continued:

> The reason I went to Jeffrey Epstein's house in the first place was the rumor was that he was throwing wild parties. Nobody knew who he was, really, at that time because it was before he took Bill Clinton on his plane. I thought, "Oh, well, let me check this out!" Then I got there and I thought, "Maybe I shouldn't check this out."
>
> I noticed there were some drugs around. I noticed girls. And I noticed a lot of married men that didn't seem to be there with their wives, which is sort of why I'm not mentioning who was there . . .
>
> In the nineties, drug use wasn't quite as common on Wall Street as it is now, or as open. I noticed at the party that people were wandering off to private rooms and God only knows what they were doing in there: drugs, women, whatever.
>
> So I said, "Oh, maybe this isn't the party scene for me."

Many of Epstein's party guests never could have guessed that what happened during the daytime at the house on El Brillo Way was even more disturbing.

In 2005, a mother called Florida's Palm Beach Police Department, frantic, claiming that her fourteen-year-old daughter had been enticed to Epstein's nearby mansion. There, the woman claimed, the teenager was paid $300 to strip to her underwear and massage the fifty-two-year-old. Her secret had been discovered when school administrators found the cash on her after a playground fight.

On her word, Detective Joseph Recarey launched a year-long undercover investigation into Epstein and exactly what was happening behind the walls of his mansion. What he found was worse than even the seasoned investigators could have imagined.

Ultimately, they spoke to thirty-four victims. The girls' stories were chilling in their similarity.

In a buried videotaped police victim interview we obtained, one skinny and skittish young woman reveals the horrible secret she'd been hiding for years.

"Every girl that meets Jeffrey starts off with giving him a massage," she said. "The more you do with him, the more you make. Basically, if you take off your clothes, you're going to make more. If you let him do things to you, you're going to make more."

"By do things, you mean touch you?" a detective asked.

"Yes, touch you in inappropriate places," she answered. "I did it naked, but I wouldn't let him touch me or anything like that. So after that, he says, 'You know what, listen, I'll pay you $200 for every girl you bring to me.'"

"It was like a train," she said. "I brought my friends, they brought their friends, and it went on and on."

"Did Jeff know anybody's real true age or he didn't care?" a detective asked.

She said, "I don't think he cared. He told me the younger, the better."

A cache of police victim interview videos obtained by *Epstein: Devil in the Darkness* reveals a chilling detail. Police entered the videos into evidence marked with the victims' birthdates. Recorded throughout 2005, the anonymous dates are a haunting reminder of just how young Epstein's victims were, even years after their abuse by Epstein:

6/1/86

8/09/86

12/30/86

9/21/86

12/30/86

2/8/87

6/6/87

6/18/87

6/30/87

10/10/87

2/29/88

3/8/88

4/19/88

4/21/88

7/28/88

One young victim recruited for Epstein by a high school friend was sixteen-year-old Michelle Licata. Licata spoke to our reporter Marjorie Hernandez, describing the horror of El Brillo Way.

"Life before Jeffrey Epstein was football games, cheerleading competitions," Licata said. "When I met Jeffrey Epstein I was, I think about sixteen years old and I had just started a job at Publix. I was a cashier. I was trying to get into a different crew of friends that I wanted to hang out with. . . . There was a girl that I went to high school with and she was part of that group."

Licata continued:

I can't remember what class we were in, but she was sitting right next to me. She was writing me a note. She asked if I wanted to make some extra money for Christmas. Having seven brothers and sisters, I thought that this is going to be the year that I'm going to get everybody something. That's exactly what I wanted to do.

She was writing me a note and said, "Do you want to make some extra money?" I was like, "Yeah! I mean, how do you do that?" She said that she's done it and that you just massage old guys. I was like, "Okay."

I was like, "Do you have to have a license, like a massage license to do that?" She said no. Then she said, "But if you tell anybody, I will kick your ass." I was like, "Okay." I didn't understand why she'd want to beat me up if I said that. Maybe she was embarrassed because she had to massage old guys, like wrinkly old men. That's the vision that I had in my head. Maybe that's why I wasn't supposed to say anything. She took the note and crumpled it up and threw it away.

I was working at Publix at the time and she came picked me up. Then she started to take me down to Palm Beach. . . . When we started going down there, I was like, "Well this would make sense. It's where rich people live. She said you can make some money. That's where you would go."

What I had envisioned in my mind was completely different than what was about to happen. I realized it when we pulled into someone's driveway. I was thinking it was going to be like a building or a facility or something where there's massage tables, but it was not like that at all.

I remember her just saying, "If somebody asks just say that you're eighteen. I don't think that they're going to ask, but just say that you are." I was like, "Okay." Once again still thinking that it's . . . You have to have a massage license. Maybe you had to be the age of eighteen to get that license? That's the way that I was thinking about it.

We walked in through the back door. . . . There was a lady, I think two ladies that walked in behind us. One kept on walking past and then one was there and she was telling me, "Hi. I'm so-and-so." I don't remember her exact name. She had a clipboard in her hand. She looked like this model, really beautiful, tall, skinny blonde girl. . . .

She told me to write down my name and my number on the counter. . . . Then she's like, "I just want you to come follow me." . . .

We walked out of the kitchen and we're going up this staircase. It was like half a spiral staircase. She was just prepping me to go into this room and she was telling me, "So the temperature's going to be cooler, Jeffrey's going to be in there. He's going to be making some phone calls. There's going to be some lotions on the counter. Just go ahead and start massaging him and just listen to what he says and what he wants you to do and just go ahead and do that." I was like, "Okay."

I went in there and there was . . . Like she said there was lotion set up on a vanity. There was already money sitting out.

Jeffrey Epstein came in and he introduced himself. He asked me what my name was and I told him, "Hi, I'm Michelle." He looked like he was about to get on the phone and just go and do business, make phone calls.

When he came into the room, he had on a towel and that was it. He had it wrapped up around him and he just walked in. He still had on the towel when he was laying on his stomach and he just got onto the phone. He said there's lotion and he set a timer. There was a timer on the table and he set that. He was asking me to . . . He got on the phone.

He was like, "Just go ahead and massage my feet." Every once in a while, "Go ahead and massage my calves. Go ahead and massage this and that." I was like okay, this seems to be normal. This would be a massage like any normal place. Then he got off the phone and he started talking to me.

That's when I knew this was going to go wrong. When he started asking me very personal questions about my sex life. He was asking me how many guys I'd ever been with. Do I have a boyfriend? You look so beautiful.

You're fighting back and forth like, "I don't understand what's really going on, but this old man is telling me to do things." Then also you don't really know who is this person, who is he? Does he have a gun? Is he going to kidnap me right now and lock me up in some kind of basement?

Then on top of it, putting his hand on my hip and spinning me, like, "Do a spin for me. Let me see what you look like." It's like okay, but you're not really sure if you said no, what would happen? That's what I was afraid of is if I say no, am I going to be killed?

What are my options for getting out of this room alive? Because so far, my mind has been wrong since pulling into a house and a driveway it has gone wrong. It just keeps getting worse and worse. We're not at this place that I thought we're going to be going to. There's one person and now he is looking at me. Now he's getting into a place into my head that is a very personal place. He is digging. He is digging in . . . That to me is worse than what he could do or touch me.

He took this really private place and he turned it into a nightmare for a really long time. It still haunts me. . . . I mean, here I am. I wrote down in my planner that I stayed on the phone until 4:00 in the morning with a boy. That's what I thought was just so awesome. Then to have or I think I wrote, I kissed so-and-so. I mean, that's where my mind was. That's the level of sexuality that I was at.

At this point I was in my bra and my underwear and I remembered the bra because it was one particular bra that I ever had really that was like that. It clipped in the front. He had popped it off. He just kept telling me he liked that and to do that. It just got more just grabby and turning me and looking at me. I just kept thinking if that timer could just hurry up, I would just really love to get out here. . . .

He knew that I was uncomfortable. He continued anyways. He was really going to town on himself. He kept going and then at one point he just, I guess finished and he jumped up, wrapped his towel around him. He said, "Okay, thank you. I would really love to see you again. There's $200 there for you. Your number and your name make sure it's downstairs before you go. I will call you and have you come back."

I was just thinking, "Oh my God, you've got to be kidding. You're out of your mind. You're out of your mind if you think I will ever be here again in my entire life."

I just went back downstairs. . . . I guess my friend saw the terror on my face. I was just freaked out and she said, "What happened?" I was like, "I will tell you in the car. Just get out of here right now. I want to go home."

We got in the car and she's like, "What?" I was like, "He was trying to finger me and stuff." She's like, "That's it? That's not a big deal. He tried to do that with my last friend."

I was like, "What's your last friend? How many people have you brought?" It was like this feeling of just being used as someone's play toy. I just put my sunglasses on and I looked out the window. It was like forty-five minutes' drive back to my car.

I was just crying without her knowing the whole way home. I was just thinking about, I don't know. How's anybody ever going to love me?

Ashamed, Licata told only her very best friend what had happened, and tried to move on. A year later, she got a visit from the police.

"I was seventeen, and some men in some black suits showed up at my house," she told Hernandez. "My brother answered the door and he was like, 'Michelle there's some men in black suits looking for you. Why?' I was like, 'I have no idea.'

I went out there and I was talking to them. They said, "Do you know Jeffrey Epstein?" I was like, "No." I thought it was some kid. I thought some kid died in school.

They kept talking and I'm trying to think of like, "Was I doing something in high school?" I was still thinking, "Who did I hang out with at school that may have wanted to hurt themselves or kill themselves?" and I was like, "What's happening?"

Then they said Palm Beach. It all just came back, rushed all through my body.

I was just like, "Oh my God. I was like, I'm in trouble. These men have found me and I'm going to go to jail." I thought I was going to jail.

I met up with them in a parking lot, which is still really sketchy, in a parking lot right next to my work. We're in their car and they had a recorder and they were recording me.

They didn't explain a whole lot, just like, "Well this has happened to other girls. It's okay you can tell us what happened." There wasn't any like, "Hey, let's get together. Why don't you come down to the station while we do this?" You would think any normal police investigation would be like fingerprints or something, or I don't know what their goal was that day, but it didn't make me feel safer to talk to them.

The police, when I was talking to them and in the car with them, they were just asking me what happened. They just wanted to know what I knew. What information I had. Do I remember anybody that was there? How did you end up there? They just asked me to tell my story to them as to what happened.

Apparently it was because there was one girl that came out and actually said something. I think she told her mom, and her mom brought it to the police's attention. Then because Jeffrey Epstein had a bunch of names and phone numbers and stuff that he had in his possession, and I think they found something of that nature and that's how they could find the girls. Because they told me that they found my name and my phone number in his house. They wanted to ask me some questions about what was happening there.

I recently just listened to the recording from that day. I remember just sounding so terrified that I was in trouble. That I was so young, I was such a little girl still when I was saying stuff. I was like, "So he was masturbating."

You could tell I didn't even really know the right words were to tell these men, these once again older men, that were recording me in a car, in a parking lot. That happened.

Then I think the FBI sent a lady to come meet up with me and we spoke together as well in the parking lot of a hospital. She recorded our conversation. It was just her and I, then I redid the story.

After I gave my statement to the Palm Beach police department and the FBI agent I was never contacted again by the law and by the justice system. I was never kept up to date as to what was going on.

It's like this really long process of literally nothing happening. It is like we're talking about this guy, we have all this evidence of what he's been doing and yet how many years has it been going on, and how long has literally nothing happened, nothing.

After a yearlong investigation, police had completed interviews with dozens of girls like Michelle. Detectives even picked through Epstein's trash and discovered incriminating messages on scraps of paper documenting phone calls.

"She is wondering if 2:30 is OK . . . She needs to stay in school," read one document obtained during the course of our investigation.

Another slip of paper suggested that Epstein had had a bouquet of roses sent to one teen at her high school following a school performance.

An Amazon packing slip addressed to Epstein that we obtained reveals he'd ordered some seriously disturbing reading material: *Slavecraft: Roadmaps for Erotic Servitude, Training with Miss Abernathy: A Workbook for Erotic Slaves*, and *SM 101: A Realistic Introduction*.

Was his sexual exploitation confined to young girls? A piece of note paper obtained by cops and recovered by our team shows that someone jotted down the urls "TonyaWorld.com" and "Trannsvicious.aol.com." The former is still live at the time of this writing, featuring "T-Girls from All Over the World," "Ethnic SheMales," "Thousands of SheMales," and "Direct Contacts" for the models on the site.

Armed with such details from their surveillance work, the police finally got the go-ahead to raid the home on El Brillo Way.

A Palm Beach Police Department incident report obtained by the authors of this book describes the scene in Det. Joseph Recarey's own words:

> As we entered onto the property, we encountered the house manager, Janusz Banasiak, who was in the guest portion of the house. . . . The members of the Police Department entered the house and announced we had a search warrant.
>
> Several interior decorators were located on the property. I spoke with Mark Zeff. . . . Mr. Zeff stated he is the designer for Mr. Epstein's homes. He advised he was contacted in March of 2005 to do a complete overhaul on the house. He advised he was on the phone with Mr. Epstein when officers announced the search warrant. Mr. Epstein was then made aware of the search warrant. . . .
>
> I entered the residence and located two covert (hidden) cameras. The first camera was a covert wall clock in the garage area. I traced the wire behind the clock and removed the RCA wire and unplugged the camera. The other covert camera was located within a desk clock beside Epstein's desk."

Epstein's unassuming home on El Brillo Way in Palm Beach was the site of his worst abuses. (The Mega Agency)

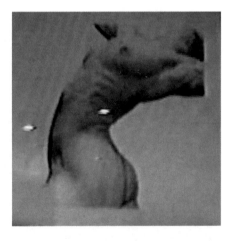

Epstein's Palm Beach home featured several images of nude women. (Palm Beach County State Attorney's Office)

This photo of a young blonde girl flashing her bare rear end at the camera was found in Epstein's Palm Beach home. This and other images from inside the home were captured during a 2005 Palm Beach police raid. (Palm Beach County State Attorney's Office)

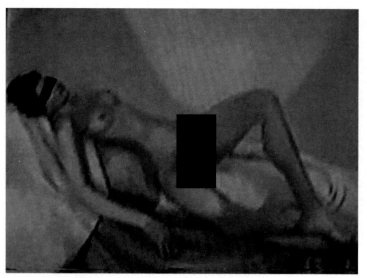

Disembodied and immobile women were a common theme of the art pieces in Epstein's Palm Beach home. (Palm Beach County State Attorney's Office)

A hand-drawn portrait of Ghislaine Maxwell overlooked the infamous massage room. (Palm Beach County State Attorney's Office)

The massage room was stocked with lotions and oils, and had a bathtub as well. (Palm Beach County State Attorney's Office)

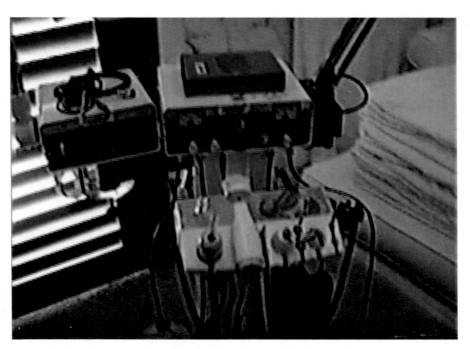

This screenshot from a Palm Beach police raid video shows the chilling "massager" and other devices alongside Epstein's massage table. (Palm Beach County State Attorney's Office)

1) car → extension
/month

2) 9^{00} pm bucket of roses
to Royal Palm Beach
High school for ████████
Give the flowers at
8:30 to sb. to
give it to her ∅ at
the stage after
performance

Jeffrey E. Epstein

Police found a note in Epstein's trash directing his assistant to deliver a "bucket of roses" to a female student at Royal Palm Beach High School. (Palm Beach County State Attorney's Office)

IMPORTANT MESSAGE

FOR: Jeffrey
DATE: 4/1/05   TIME: 8:08 A.M.
M: Jean - Luc
OF:
PHONE/MOBILE: ██████████

TELEPHONED	✓	PLEASE CALL	
CAME TO SEE YOU		WILL CALL AGAIN	
WANTS TO SEE YOU		RUSH	
RETURNED YOUR CALL		SPECIAL ATTENTION	

MESSAGE: He has a teacher
for you to teach you
how to speak russian.
She is 2x8 years old
not blonde. Lessons are
free and you can
have 1st today if you
call

SIGNED: _____ 1184

IMPORTANT MESSAGE

FOR: JE
DATE: _____   TIME: 5:14 P.M.
M: JeanLuc
OF:
PHONE/MOBILE:

TELEPHONED		PLEASE CALL	
CAME TO SEE YOU		WILL CALL AGAIN	
WANTS TO SEE YOU		RUSH	
RETURNED YOUR CALL		SPECIAL ATTENTION	

MESSAGE: ("just did a good
one - 18 years -
she spoke to me & said
"I love Jeffrey")

SIGNED: _____ 1184

A phone message for Jeffrey Epstein, from Jean-Luc Brunel. (Palm Beach County State Attorney's Office)

A phone message for Jeffrey Epstein, from Jean-Luc Brunel. (Palm Beach County State Attorney's Office)

A photo of girls in a massage chain, found inside Epstein's Palm Beach home. (Palm Beach County State Attorney's Office)

> In my quietest moments I Flick back to these memories I have of degrading my body and morals and I fill up with agony knowing I participated in acts I would never wish on any ~~young lady.~~

Sex slave Victoria Roberts recorded her own personal nightmare in a secret diary. (American Media)

> The entire affair was short-lived, when his climax was achieved he was not the same attentive guy I had known for the last few hours. Instead he quickly got dressed, said his good-byes and slipped out of my bedroom to the driver still waiting for him outside.

Virginia Roberts' diaries were later submitted as evidence to the court. (American Media)

The Lolita Express bedroom featured a locking door. (The Mega Agency)

Other areas of the Lolita Express looked more like a normal private jet. (The Mega Agency)

According to Donald Trump, his friendship with Epstein stretches back to the 1980s. (The Mega Agency)

Donald Trump, Melania Trump, Prince Andrew, Epstein, and Ghislaine (L to R) all partied together at Mar-a-Lago in 2000. (The Mega Agency)

Victoria Roberts photographed with Prince Andrew and Ghislaine Maxwell. (Palm Beach County State Attorney's Office)

Flight logs like these ones exposed the extent of Epstein's relationships with the rich and powerful. (American Media)

Detective Joseph Recarey had actually been inside Epstein's home before: back on October 5, 2003, when Epstein accused "a former disgruntled house-man" of stealing money from the house. He described what his team expected to find in his October 18, 2005, Affidavit & Application for Search Warrant, obtained by this team: "I observed several covert cameras, which would capture and record images of anyone within the residence. Epstein had purchased covert cameras which were built in wall clocks and table clocks. These images were then downloaded onto a proprietary spyware software for later viewing."

Recarey noted that Epstein "told me that he had purchased a spy camera from a store on Okeechobee Blvd. and had set up the camera which was in a clock in his office."

Indeed, when they got permission and raided the home on October 20, 2005, they found a trove of files and recording materials. Evidence logs obtained by this team catalog the haul:

- 12 phone message books, filled with names and messages from his famous friends
- 3 file folders of similar messages, ripped off of pads
- 1 bag of shredded paper, found in his office
- 1 orange folder marked "Massages"
- More than 123 photographs
- 4 VHS tapes
- 2 CDs marked "Happy birthday"
- 63 CDs
- 1 DVD
- 16 Zip CDs
- 12 8mm video tapes
- 5 memory cards, as would be used in a digital camera
- 11 floppy disks

- 1 zip drive
- 3 computer CPUs
- 1 Maxell CD-R

They also found other items that hinted at the depravity the house had hosted:

- 4 massage tables
- 1 black framed photo of a nude girl
- 1 green framed photo of a nude girl
- 2 twin torpedo vibrators
- 1 bottle of joy jelly
- 3 X-rated videotapes: *Sex In City*, *Eat in Janine*, and *I Love Lesbians Four*
- Penis- and vagina-shaped soaps
- 1 school transcript

Still, something seemed off. Epstein's pals, interior decorator and architect Douglas Schoettle were there when the raid occurred, and seemed unperturbed. The materials they managed to get their hands on weren't a slam dunk for conviction. Some of Epstein's recording devices and computers had been removed, cords left hanging when cops arrived. Had Epstein been tipped off?

"The place had been cleaned up," former detective Michael Reiter later told *NBC News*.

Still, by May 2006, Detective Recarey believed the case was bulletproof.

Recarey amassed a Probable Cause Affidavit filled with damning evidence against Epstein. The official document even included a description of Epstein's distorted genitalia.

"It was thick towards the bottom but was thin and small towards the head portion," a victim said, calling it, "egg-shaped."

Another victim told cops it's "like a teardrop."

"It's really fat at the bottom and skinny at the top," she continued, making reference to "some sort of birth defect on his thing."

But once the case got into the hands of the higher ups, the case did not proceed how the cops were expecting.

According to Reiter, Epstein's high-powered defense team, which included Kenneth Starr and Alan Dershowitz, seemed to know details about the cops' case even before they emerged. (Starr was best known for heading an investigation of members of the Clinton administration; Dershowitz for serving on the legal "Dream Team" alongside Johnnie Cochran and F. Lee Bailey in the 1995 O. J. Simpson murder trial.)

"We believed that the content of our probable cause affidavit eventually, some time after we presented it to the state attorney's office, ended up with the defense attorneys," Reiter said.

"Because minute details that nobody else knew that were in those documents were being refuted and contrary information provided by the defense."

Furious, Reiter demanded that the state attorney, Barry Krischer, remove himself from the case. That didn't go anywhere, so Recary brought the Department's evidence to the FBI.

When it became clear that the federal probe would encounter similar roadblocks, Reiter arranged a meeting with the prosecutor in charge of the case, US Attorney Alex Acosta: President Trump's future secretary of labor.

Acosta put on a good show. Reiter said, "I left that meeting thinking, 'This guy hopefully is going to do his job.'"

Reiter would be wrong.

CHAPTER 9
EPSTEIN: IN THE VICTIMS' OWN WORDS

Police Victim Interview A

Police: Pepsi's coming! First of all, I know you're freaking out. Don't freak out, just relax. I understand you may have information on a case that we're looking into.
Victim: I'm not gonna get in trouble for anything I say, right? . . .

P: How do you make money with Jeffrey?
V: There's two ways. . . . Every girl that meets Jeffrey starts off with giving him a massage. The more you do with him, the more you make. Basically, if you take off your clothes, you're gonna make more. If you let him do things to you, you're gonna make more . . . touch you in inappropriate places . . . He uses his hands, and I wouldn't really call it a vibrator, I guess like a massager. I did it naked, but I wouldn't let him touch me or anything like that. My friend told me that she knew a girl that slept with him and made $1000.

So after that he's like, "You know what? I'll pay you $200 for every girl that you bring to me. I don't want you to massage me anymore, just bring girls to me."

So for every girl that I brought to Jeffrey, I would make $200.

He would tell me make sure these girls know what to expect, what they want. Because when I get into that room, they need to know.

[One girl] came to me saying she needed money. . . . I basically told her about it and she was like, "Um what do you have to do?" I told her, I was like, "The more you do, the more you make."

You're gonna take your clothes off. But the more you do, the more you make.

She gave him a massage and she basically let him like touch her, down there . . . When she got in the car I was like, "How much did you make?" and she said, $300, and I just knew right then that she did more. I asked her like, "What did you do?" She's like, "Well I started doing the massage and my clothes came off, and he put his fingers inside me." . . .

P: How old were you when you were approached to go see Jeffrey?
V: Umm . . . 16 or 17.

P: How many girls have you brought to him?
V: Oh . . . a lot.

P: Who else was underage?
V: What do you mean, like under 18? All of them.

P: Did Jeff know anybody's real true age, or did he care?

V: I don't think he cared. He told me, the younger the better. I tried to bring him a woman who was 23 and he didn't really like it . . .

Police Victim Interview B

V: It was in high school, everybody was trying to make money. I had two jobs.

P: Do you have any formal massage training?

V: No . . . It seems really weird, the whole situation. There were more girls in the house. And then we just go upstairs it was a massage room and he came like you know and I give him a massage.

P: Did you recall anything weird when you were going up the stairs?

V: The pictures.

P: Pictures of what?

V: Naked people . . .

V: I sit down there and she tells me, "Just wait a second." So she comes back and we put down the little bed for the massage. And she's like, "OK there's some lotion and he'll be right out." So he comes in and says, "OK . . . just a massage." He took his clothes off, and he was in like a towel.

P: At any point did he ask you to remove your clothes?

V: Yeah. And I say no. [sic]

P: So you continue with the massage?

V: Yeah. It was kind of weird I guess.

P: How much did he pay you?

V: $200.

P: During the time that you're massaging him on his chest, is he touching himself?

V: Yes . . . Well you know he started getting a little excited. And he started touching himself and I told him to stop.

P: You mean by touching himself, you mean he was masturbating?

V: Yes. He like had his hand under the towel. . . .

P: He offered you more money to get naked?

V: Yes. Well, he told me just to take my shirt off. I was just scared that he was going to do something.

P: Did you ever get naked while doing the massages?

V: Once, but it was in my underwear. It was never completely naked. I think there was one where I took my bra off, but that was it. He offered me more money if I have [sic] sex with him, and I said that's never gonna happen. It's not what I'm gonna do for money.

P: Did he offer you more to do more things?

V: Yah. $100 more just to take my shirt off. He tried to talk to you just to make you comfortable with the situation. Like go where are you working. How much do you make at your work. He starts saying you can make more with me. I didn't feel like it was right.

Police Victim Interview C

V: She took me over to the house. She waited downstairs. I just went upstairs and gave him a massage and that was it. She's like oh do you know do you need to make any extra money. . . . This older guy in Palm Beach, he gets a lot of massages from girls. He asked me to take my shirt off, so I took my shirt off.

P: So, were you in a bra or were you topless?
V: I ended up being topless, yeah . . . for a while I was doing it like once a week for a few months. Probably somewhere around there . . .

P: Did you ever take your panties off and be completely nude?
V: Every now and then yeah.

P: He touch himself?
V: Yes . . . he would masturbate

P: Did you ever bring anybody to the house?
V: Yes I did. Neither one of them wanted to go back though.

Police Victim Interview D

V: I was short on rent one month and she told me all I had to do was give him a massage and he would give me $200. . . . I thought about it

and I was like I really need the money. I asked
my parents and they couldn't give me the money.
I asked everyone I knew. So, I went there, and
I gave him the massage and it was a weird
situation.

P: Did you provide the massage with clothing
on?

V: All I had was underwear on. She did not tell
me that. I was absolutely surprised when I got
there. I knew nothing. He had a towel over his
private parts and he was just laying on a table
and I was just massaging from the knee down for
about 45 minutes . . . . ten minutes before we
were getting ready to leave he asked her to
leave because we were in the room together, and
he asked me to massage his chest and he had the
towel on. And about 5 minutes into it he took
the towel off and started pleasing himself,
which I was very uncomfortable with. Like I
wanted to leave right when I got there.

I'm sorry I don't like thinking back on it, it
was so . . .

When he started pleasing himself he got up and
went over to a drawer and he pulled out this
vibrator thing and then he pulled down my
panties . . . it was like this stick with a
knob on it. He didn't like stick it inside me
but he put it on me.

He just got up and walked out. He's like, "OK
you can put your clothes on," and he closed the

door. After he walked out and when I went out, I went downstairs and he was down there and there were like there other girls there. I guess they stayed there or something.

P: Did he say anything to you while you were doing the massage?

V: He was talking about art and everything like that and you know just the paintings on the walls that he had and stuff like that. The whole situation was odd. Before we even got out of the car when we just pulled up she said, "Don't say anything. Don't speak unless you're spoken to." So I was like, "What the hell are you getting me into?" So, I didn't say anything and there were pictures, pencil drawings of naked people. It looked really weird. . . . I am so ashamed that I did that because it's not like me . . .

Police Victim Interview E

V: I told her that I didn't want to be left alone with someone because I was molested when I was 12, so just like me being alone like right now I'm kinda uncomfortable and I told her that like I'm not going if you're not gonna be there with me and I was unaware that I was gonna be alone with him for that ten minutes and I thought I was gonna die . . .

Jane Doe #1: An anonymous victim who spoke in court against Epstein on August 27, 2019, seventeen days after his death.

"I still feel like I am learning the ways that he's impacted me.

"Even though Jeffrey Epstein brought it to a grand scale, on some level, a lot of girls could relate to the trauma we are talking about."

Jane Doe #2: An anonymous victim who spoke in court against Epstein on August 27, 2019, seventeen days after his death

"I think each of us has a different story and different circumstances for why we stayed in it, but for me, I think he was really strategic in how he approached each of us. Things happened slowly over time. It was almost like that analogy of a frog being in a pan of water and slowly turning the flame up.

"A lot of us were in very vulnerable situations and in extreme poverty, circumstances where we didn't have anyone on our side."

Jane Doe #3: An anonymous victim who spoke in court against Epstein on August 27, 2019, seventeen days after his death

"My world kind of spiraled after that. I stopped going on modeling castings. I gained weight. I became depressed. I stopped going out with my friends. And only five months after I had been in New York City to pursue my dream, I left. I left the modeling industry, I left New York City, and I totally switched my career path."

Jane Doe #4: An anonymous victim who spoke in court against Epstein on August 27, 2019, seventeen days after his death

"We will always carry irreparable damage and pain throughout our lives after this. It's something that's never going to go away. Whoever we marry in our life, whatever future we have in our life, it's always going to be something that's always there for us."

Jane Doe #5: An anonymous victim who spoke in court against Epstein on August 27, 2019, seventeen days after his death

"You paid for your freedom. You violated my rights. You should have to pay for them, just as anyone else. You got a plea deal no one else would have been able to get. You used your money to get out of paying the price for your actions."

Jane Doe #6: An anonymous victim who spoke in court against Epstein on August 27, 2019, seventeen days after his death

"Jeffrey Epstein stole my innocence. He gave me a life sentence of guilt and shame. I do not consider myself a victim. I see myself a survivor."

Jane Doe #7: An anonymous victim who spoke in court against Epstein on August 27, 2019, seventeen days after his death

"I used to be relatively carefree, inquisitive, hopeful, and excited about life, but my life changed because of Jeffrey Epstein. My perspective on life became very dark when I was unknowingly recruited by one of his agents. Jeffrey Epstein ruined me."

Jane Doe #8: An anonymous victim who spoke in court against Epstein on August 27, 2019, seventeen days after his death

"I cannot say that I am pleased he committed suicide, but I am at peace knowing he will not be able to hurt anyone else. However, the sad truth remains. I, along with other people, will never have an answer as to why. I will never have an apology for the wrongdoing. And most importantly, Epstein will not be justly sentenced for his crimes."

Jane Doe #9: An anonymous victim who spoke in court against Epstein on August 27, 2019, seventeen days after his death

"When I was fifteen years old, I flew on Jeffrey Epstein's plane to Zorro Ranch, where I was sexually molested by him for many hours. What I remember most vividly was him explaining to me how beneficial the experience was for me and how much he was helping me to grow.

"I remember feeling so small and powerless, especially after he positioned me by laying me on his floor so that I was confronted by all the framed photographs on his dresser of him smiling with wealthy celebrities and politicians."

Jane Doe #10: An anonymous victim who spoke in court against Epstein on August 27, 2019, seventeen days after his death

"Epstein targeted and took advantage of me, a young girl, whose mother had recently died a horrific death and whose family structure had deteriorated. His actions placed me, a young girl, into a downward spiral to the point where I purchased a gun and drove myself to an isolated place to end my suffering."

Jane Doe #11: An anonymous victim who spoke in court against Epstein on August 27, 2019, seventeen days after his death

"He promised me that he would write me a letter of recommendation for Harvard if I got the grades and scores needed for admission. His word was worth a lot, he assured me, as he was in the midst of funding and leading Harvard's studies on the human brain, and the president was his friend.

"I had never even kissed a boy before I met him, and never throughout the horrific abuse did Jeffrey Epstein kiss me even once. When he stole my virginity, he washed my entire body compulsively in the shower and then told me, 'If you're not a virgin, I will kill you.' And then I wasn't a virgin anymore."

Jane Doe #12: An anonymous victim who spoke in court against Epstein on August 27, 2019, seventeen days after his death

"They told me to go upstairs and directed me to Jeffrey Epstein's office. Mr. Epstein had a white robe on and we chatted very briefly. I had my portfolio of photos, but he didn't even look at it. Suddenly, he took his robe off and got close to me. I got up to leave, but the door was locked."

Chauntae Davies

"I began my massage, trying not to let him smell my fear and obvious discomfort, but before I knew what was happening, he grabbed onto my wrist and tugged me towards the bed. I tried to pull away, but he was unbuttoning my shorts and pulling my body onto his already naked body faster than I could think. I was searching for words but all I could say was, 'No, please stop,' but that just seemed to excite him more."

Marijke Chartouni

"She told me he went to Cooper Union. He was a mathematical genius. That he had favorite girls that he would take to Chanel for fifteen-minute, all-you-can-buy shopping trips. She told me his right-hand person had connection to the arts and the fashion world, and she could help me."

Jennifer Araoz

"He robbed me of my dreams. He robbed me of my chance to pursue a career I always adored. He stole my chance at really feeling love because I was so scared to trust anyone for so many years that I had such severe anxiety. I didn't want to leave my house, let alone my bed.

"The fact that I will never have a chance to face my predator in court eats away at my soul. Even in death, Epstein is trying to hurt me. I had hoped to at last get an apology, but this evil man had no remorse or caring for what he did to anyone."

Alicia Arden

"He was touching my hips and my butt, and wanting to lift my skirt up. He said he wanted to manhandle me. I filed a police report but I really wasn't taken seriously. My family, my friends discouraged me because I wasn't physically raped. I was assaulted, he was touching me and taking my clothes off, and I felt if I didn't get out of there it could've been worse.

"So did it need to be worse? Did I need to be raped for anyone to take me seriously?"

Teala Davies

"I was going to start this statement by saying that I was a victim of Jeffrey Epstein. But that's not the case. I'm still a victim of Jeffrey Epstein. I'm still a victim because the fear of not being heard stopped me from telling my story for so many years. . . . I'm still a victim because I am fearful for my daughters and everyone's daughters. . . . I'm still a victim because the seventeen-year-old Teala was manipulated into thinking she had found someone who cared, someone who wanted to help."

Courtney Wild

"Jeffrey Epstein robbed myself and all the other victims of our day in court to confront him one by one, and for that he is a coward."

Anouska De Georgiou

"Something I think is very important to communicate is that loss of innocence, trust, and joy that is not recoverable. The abuse, spanning several years, was devaluing beyond measure and affected my ability to form and maintain healthy relationships, both in my work and my personal life. He could not begin to fathom what he took from us."

Michelle Licata

"What happened to me occurred many years ago when I was in high school, but it still affects my life. I was told then that Jeffrey Epstein was going to be held accountable, but he was not. In fact, the government worked out a secret deal and didn't tell me about it. . . . The fact that I mattered this time and the other victims mattered is what counts."

Theresa J. Helm

"That experience for the last seventeen years has been a dark corner in my story. . . . So I'm here today because it is time to bring light to that darkness, and it's time to replace that darkness with light."

Virginia Roberts Giuffre

"He will not have his day in court, but the reckoning of accountability has begun, supported by the voices of these brave and beautiful women in this courtroom today. The reckoning must not end—it must continue. He did not act alone and we, the victims, know that."

Sarah Ransome

"I would like to acknowledge and extend my gratitude to the prosecutors from the Southern District of New York for pursuing justice on behalf of the victims. Please, please finish what you have started.

"We, the victims, are still here, prepared to tell the truth, and we all know he did not act alone. We are survivors, and the pursuit of justice should not abate."

Annie Farmer (Speaking on behalf of her sister Maria Farmer)

"Jeffrey Epstein and Ghislaine Maxwell not only assaulted her, but as we're hearing from so many of these brave women here today, they stole her dreams and her livelihood. She risked her safety in 1996, so many years ago, to report them—to no avail—and it is heartbreaking to her and to me that all this destruction has been wrought since that time."

CHAPTER 10

"HE'S INTELLIGENCE"

More than "34 confirmed minors" had found the bravery to share the details of their darkest nightmares with strange men in police uniforms. Jeffrey Epstein's employees had stood up to share what they knew, even though their livelihoods were at stake. The Palm Beach Police Department had put together one of the strongest and most jaw-dropping cases in recent memory, proudly passing it off to prosecutors.

Then, there was a fumble. Or more accurately, an entirely new play began to unfold behind the scenes.

United States Attorney Alex Acosta had personally assured Detective Reiter of the Palm Beach Police Department that he was on the case. The only problem, Acosta said, was that he'd simply been stymied in his efforts to bring Epstein to justice by the maneuverings of his legal team since delivering the fifty-three-page indictment that charged him with grooming, paying, and coercing underage girls to have sex with him.

Victory for the victims was still in their grasp, but Acosta had his own plans.

In October 2007, the *Miami Herald* reported, Acosta secretly met with one of Epstein's attorneys, Jay Lefkowitz, over breakfast at the Marriott in West Palm Beach. Amid vacationers and traveling businessmen, they struck one of the most outrageous sweetheart deals of all time.

According to the sentencing document obtained by this team, Epstein would:

1. Plead guilty to minor felony state charges of "Procuring a person under 18 for prostitution."
2. Epstein and "any potential co-conspirators" would be immune from such charges moving forward.
3. Epstein would agree to register as a sex offender.

According to the sentencing document, the nature of Epstein's charges would have required a "lowest possible prison sentence" of 21.5 months. Instead, that document showed Epstein would serve twelve months in prison and ten months of probation. A box was checked noting that this was a "mitigated departure," or a decision to impose less severe penalties than the sentencing guidelines recommended. Ultimately, the final sentence was eighteen months.

The facts of that plea deal are by this point in time widely known. What most people don't realize, however, is that Palm Beach County prosecutors actually had offered Epstein another plea deal back in 2006. An even sweeter deal, it would have helped him avoid grand jury proceedings and jail time altogether, likely sweeping the entire investigation under the rug. The plea deal, issued in a letter from Assistant State Attorney Lanna Behlohlavek to Epstein's attorney Guy Fronstin and obtained by this team reads:

> By this letter, I am confirming the offer of settlement to your client, Jeffrey Epstein. Should you accept this settlement, the state will not proceed with Grand Jury proceedings tomorrow.
>
> Plea to Aggravated Assault with the Intent to Commit a Felony, a third degree felony.
>
> Adjudication will be withheld, and your client will be placed on 5 year probation with the following conditions: no contact direct or indirect with victim [redacted]; no contact with minors unless supervised by an approved adult with knowledge of the underlying facts, but in no case shall the supervising adult be

[assistants] Nadia Marcinkova or Sarah Kellen; psycho-sexual evaluation and successful completion of any recommended treatment . . . ; full payment of the costs of the investigation by the Palm Beach Police Department; and may apply for early termination of probation after three years if there are no violations.

Epstein rejected the deal. What part of that list of demands was too much for him? Was he confident at that time that he'd skate entirely?

Even when he was finally sentenced to prison, in 2008, he seemed nonplussed by the whole situation. Relaxing on Little St. James at the time, Epstein told a *New York Times* reporter that he fancied himself a real-life Gulliver, shipwrecked in a world that was so much smaller than he was.

"Gulliver's playfulness had unintended consequences," Epstein said. "That is what happens with wealth. There are unexpected burdens as well as benefits."

"I am not blameless," he admitted. Although his lawyers insisted Epstein was unaware of the girls' ages, he claimed he'd taken steps to ensure no improprieties would take place in the future.

He told the *Times* he'd hired a full-time, male masseur to replace his roster of teens. He said he'd assembled a "board of directors of friends to counsel him on his behavior." Considering the behavior of his "friends" at that moment in time—and that they were essentially the coconspirators that allowed him to get away with the worst of crimes—one could make a reasonable case that wasn't the best idea.

Heading off to prison in Miami, Epstein confessed he was "anxious" but confident: "Your body can be contained," he told the reporter, "but not your mind."

In yet another sign of his arrogance, he set his email to auto-reply, alerting friends that he was "on vacation."

In truth, Epstein's time behind bars would be more of a retreat than retribution. To start, he was not sent to federal prison like most sex offenders in the state. Instead, he was given a private wing at the Palm Beach County

Stockade Facility, where he enjoyed the care of his own personal security guards.

Even then, remarkably, he spent little time within the confines of the jail. Just over three months into his sentence, Epstein was granted work release, allowing him to leave the premises for up to seven days a week, up to sixteen hours at a time. That period included up to two hours at his Palm Beach sex den.

In principle, it was shocking. In practice, it was illegal. Florida law prohibits anyone who has committed three violations in five years from being granted work-release. Epstein pleaded guilty to charges involving one victim. But in 2018, the Southern Florida Assistant US Attorney, Maria Villafaña, announced that she'd found "inaccuracies and omissions" in Epstein's work-release file, claiming that he had actually made three violations and therefore should not have ever been given release.

What's more, of more than twenty inmates on work release at that time in the same prison, Epstein was the only sex offender.

Disturbingly, he could have used that time to commit even more crimes. South Florida's *Sun Sentinel* newspaper reported that they found more than one instance in which Epstein was not under the direct supervision of guards. What's more, there is no record of who visited him when he was "working" at a nondescript West Palm Beach office building, because those logs have been destroyed.

There are records, however, of who visited him in prison. Although a department memo had barred Epstein from seeing "family members, girlfriends, children, friends or minors," there are recorded visits by Sarah Kellen and Nadia Marcinkova. Both women have been identified in federal court as two of his potential "co-conspirators."

Kellen, who sometimes goes by Sarah Kensington or Sarah Vickers, was described as the "lieutenant" in one lawsuit, just below Ghislaine in the chain of command. In multiple lawsuits, she has been accused of scheduling girls for sex sessions with Epstein in his Palm Beach mansion. The involvement of Marcinkova, who later used the last name Marcinko, is somewhat curious. Police records show that investigators had indications that

Marcinkova might have been underage herself when she became involved with Epstein and declined to answer questions about the sex scheme when she was deposed in a lawsuit, invoking the Fifth Amendment. Her lawyers later said she was one of his victims.

Miami Herald reporters Sarah Blaskey and Nicholas Nehamas found that Epstein even made a prison commissary purchase that seemed like a likely gift for a guest: two pairs of small women's panties, size 5. Too small to fit an average adult woman, however, they certainly weren't for Kellen or Marcinkova. . . .

As for all crooks, Epstein found, there was a workaround that could make life in prison tolerable: Corruption. Epstein paid a pretty penny for his privileges.

According to records obtained by these authors, one of his nonprofit organizations paid $128,000 to the Palm Beach County Sheriff's Department to cover the cost of his personal detail. They were even known to refer to him as "the client" instead of as "the perp."

Ultimately, Epstein—one of the sickest sex fiends to ever walk the planet—only served thirteen months before he was released on "good behavior."

Overall, it was outrageous. At the time of this writing, the Florida Department of Law Enforcement is conducting an investigation into how his case was handled. Florida State Senator Lauren Brook was one of the forces behind the inquest.

"Epstein enjoyed an unprecedented and deeply troubling level of leniency and luxury while incarcerated," she said. "We need answers if we want accountability."

So, who was responsible for Epstein's incredible, once-in-a-lifetime sweetheart deal?

Then–US Attorney Alex Acosta has insisted it wasn't him. Acosta was asked about his role in the debacle while being vetted by Trump's transition team, before taking up his position as Secretary of Labor. He insisted he'd only had one meeting about the deal, according to reporter Vicky Ward—a claim that matches the *Miami Herald*'s reporting on the West Palm Beach Marriott breakfast rendezvous.

Acosta had "been told to back off," because Epstein was "above his pay-grade," Ward wrote, that "Epstein 'belonged to intelligence' . . . and to leave it alone."

But exactly who was the "intelligence" agency pulling the strings? Epstein's plea deal mysteriously hinted at the "valuable consideration" he'd been given for information he'd provided to federal prosecutors behind the scenes. The nature of that information has never been made public, and many assume that it is connected to his work as a federal witness in the prosecution of individuals connected to the 2008 collapse of his former employer, Bear Stearns.

However, also in 2008, several of Epstein's famous associates were involved in even more pressing international crises.

George W. Bush was entering the final months of his oversight of the bungled Iraq War, and Britain was one of the country's last remaining allies as part of the much-fêted Coalition of the Willing, referring to the US-led Multi-National Force in Iraq. Surely, he had reason to keep Epstein quiet, and to prevent Prince Andrew's name from being dragged through the mud in a highly publicized and scandalous trial.

In addition, former pal Bill Clinton's wife Hillary was in the midst of her first presidential campaign. Epstein's Palm Beach pal Donald Trump had even come out to support her, calling her a "wonderful woman" who would make a great president. As for Trump, he had just launched *Celebrity Apprentice*, and was riding high in his new career as a reality television star.

Also in 2008, Mohammed bin Salman had finished college and was launching his political career in Saudi Arabia by joining the Saudi Cabinet.

Notorious Saudi arms trader Adnan Khashoggi was in the midst of a reputation overhaul. "Selling an image," the *New York Times* reported at the time, " he prefers these days to be remembered as 'Mr. Fix-It' rather than the arms dealer involved in the Iran-Contra scandal."

All of these people would have had an incentive and motivation to keep the peace when it came to Epstein—and what he knew.

"Epstein was sort of flying very important people around the world, providing young girls for some of them," said author Martin Dillon, after conversations with sources in the Mossad. "Building files. It's how the intelligence services work."

"They call it the honey trap," Dillon said, referring to the time-honored intelligence practice of spies using the lure of sex to entrap targets. "But it's much more sophisticated than that."

The honey trap—or "love trap," as it is sometimes known—has a long and salacious history in American espionage. According to a 1975 *Washington Post* report, "For years, the Central Intelligence Agency operated love traps in New York and San Francisco, where foreign diplomats were lured by prostitutes in the pay of the CIA."

"Through hidden one-way mirrors, CIA agents filmed the sexual adventures and later tried to blackmail the victims into becoming informants."

The article noted, "The CIA possibly got the idea from the Russians, who have long used sex blackmail to entrap Westerners into spying for them."

CIA reps told the *Washington Post* reporters that they "had never heard of this." But for Epstein, the playbook was already written.

Dillon explained:

> If you're an intelligence community, and you have someone like Epstein, who's kind of a celebrity, who can attract celebrities, who can be in part of conversations about world events about the most secret things. If you could put people like Clinton on his planes and you can put Ehud Barak, a former Prime Minister of Israel and a former general, then he is a guy who really matters to you.
>
> If he is going to be your friend, he is going to work for you. He is going to be an asset for you. Look what he can do. He can give you information on all those politicians; on their private behavior, their peccadilloes, all these things are important to intelligence communities.

Former CIA counterterrorism specialist Philip Giraldi said he also has "little doubt" that Epstein was running an intelligence operation, and that his knowledge helped him escape justice.

"There is no other viable explanation for his filming of prominent politicians and celebrities having sex with young girls," Giraldi wrote in the *American Herald Tribune* in August 2019. "Epstein clearly had contact with former Israeli Prime Minister Shimon Peres and Ehud Barak and [Epstein's client Leslie] Wexner also had close ties to Israel and its government."

In addition to flying on the Lolita Express, former Israeli Prime Minister Ehud Barak also visited Epstein at his Manhattan home. In January 2016, he was photographed entering the property, followed by four young women soon after.

"I was there, for lunch or chat, nothing else. So what?" said Barak in a statement when the visit was reported. "I never attended a party with him. I never met Epstein in the company of women or young girls." He also admitted to having visited Little St. James, but said he did not attend any parties or see any young girls there either.

According to Giraldi, former Palm Beach County state attorney Barry Krischer also may have been responsible for swaying Acosta in 2008, behind-the-scenes. Krischer had won the prestigious Anti-Defamation League (ADL) Award ten years before. (The ADL is a US-based Jewish organization with a long history of domestic spying allegations.)

"The Jewish state regularly tops the list for ostensibly friendly countries that aggressively conduct espionage against the US," Giraldi claimed. "Mossad would have exploited Epstein's contacts. . . . Those blackmailed would undoubtedly in most cases cooperate with the foreign government involved to avoid a major scandal."

Fallen into the hands of the American justice system in Florida, he could have provided information far more explosive than whatever was happening at Bear Stearns.

Indeed, Epstein's attorney Kenneth Starr at one point went over Acosta's head to Republican appointees at the Department of Justice, demanding that they drop the case. The attorney general in 2008, who likely would have received the request, was Michael Mukasey—an Orthodox Jew with such deep ties to Israel, that he has been accused of having dual citizenship.

In retrospect, it's clear that Epstein's blackmail files were at the heart of his epic sweetheart deal. It wasn't just the contents of those files that his friends and enemies wanted kept quiet, however. It was the fact that the deal itself seemed most dangerous.

As part of the plea deal, Acosta and his team agreed to try to keep the details of their arrangement out of the press. The *New York Times* covered Epstein's sentencing in a fluffy report set on his "palm-fringed Xanadu in the Caribbean."

"To prosecutors, Mr. Epstein is just another sex offender," reporter Landon Thomas Jr. insisted, despite all evidence to the contrary. Epstein "admits" that "his behavior was inappropriate," Thomas wrote—perhaps in the understatement of the century. The article even featured tough talk from a member of Acosta's team insisting that Epstein would get no house arrest, a claim that Thomas apparently did not question.

It was later revealed that Thomas had asked Epstein for a $30,000 donation to his favored charity. After the donation was uncovered, Thomas left the *New York Times* under a cloud of controversy.

Even worse than the media secrecy that surrounded the deal was the fact that it was deliberately hidden from the victims. A letter from one of Epstein's attorneys to Acosta makes the plot clear: As part of the plea deal, Acosta would be barred from informing "any of the identified individuals, potential witnesses or potential civil claimants" about the details or even the existence of the agreement.

Spencer Kuvin was an attorney representing several Epstein victims at the time. He described how he and his clients were kept in the dark to veteran crime reporter Doug Montero.

"I'm in the courtroom and Mr. Epstein pleads guilty," Kuvin recalled." At this point, we still don't know on behalf the victims what he's pleading guilty to. We don't know how long he's going to stay in jail, we don't know what the non-prosecution agreement that he entered into says, what it says for the victims, what it says about him, what charges he's admitting to or what is the standard of all of the allegations that he's admitting to at the time. He's just whisked off and that's it."

He continued:

> We go back to our offices and I call the US Attorney's Office and they still don't give us any information. They don't tell us what he pleaded guilty to, they don't even tell us that there's a non-prosecution agreement. I learned about it later, on behalf of my client through, again, a source that tells me, 'Hey, did you know that there's a document out there that's a non-prosecution agreement that you should get ahold of because it effectively talks about your clients and certain victims that he's pleading guilty to.
>
> As attorneys, there were about four or five of us at the time representing various different victims to get ahold of this non-prosecution agreement. Mr. Epstein's lawyers fought us and wouldn't produce it, refused to produce the agreement. We had to go to court and over a period of a year, this is one year after the federal government enters into an agreement with Mr. Epstein to not prosecute him, essentially having him plead guilty to the same exact charges that these girls have accused him of.
>
> We, on behalf of the victims still don't have the agreement and the judge finally orders that it be produced to the victims. They then, on behalf of Mr. Epstein, appeal that decision from the judge. So we still don't get a copy of it until it goes through the appellate court system, which lasts another six to seven months before we finally, ultimately get ahold of this deal.
>
> We see when we open the deal and take a look at it, that it gives immunity to not only Mr. Epstein but also his coconspirators, some which are specifically named. Then in the language of the

document, it includes any and all potential other coconspirators in this non-prosecution agreement.

So the federal government enters into a deal, which essentially gives not only Mr. Epstein immunity but all of the other people that potentially could have been coconspirators bringing women or girls to his home. It was an unbelievable deal.

We had never seen something so broad before, we had no idea why they would enter into such a deal. What was the motivation? Why would you give this man such a deal like this?

You know, if this had been Joe Plumber working in Palm Beach and had abused one minor, two minors, he could be sitting behind bars for sixty to seventy years. This is a man that had abused probably over forty young girls, and now you're giving them this deal and giving immunity to all those coconspirators? It just never made any sense.

None of it made sense. The speed with which they entered into the deal, the breadth or the scope of the investigation, which, by the way, didn't even go outside of Palm Beach at the time. For some unknown reason, the US Attorney's Office, Mr. Acosta, decided to keep it within Palm Beach. It just never made any sense.

The only thing that we could think on behalf of the young girls was that maybe Mr. Epstein had traded information and given the federal government information that nobody knew about, that they weren't telling us. . . . But we never knew because they wouldn't tell us, and they wouldn't tell the victims.

In this case, it seemed, silence was golden. But who would benefit from Epstein keeping his mouth shut?

CHAPTER 11

THE HUNT FOR JUSTICE

Months and even years after the sexual assaults that changed their lives, Epstein's victims stood in the shadows, trying to move on with their lives while also awaiting the justice that would allow them to do so—justice that would never come

Attorneys like Spencer Kuvin who had stood by them through the investigation began to help them file civil suits in an attempt to find some kind of closure.

"After the FBI conducted all of their investigations, and talked to all of these young women, by then, some of these women had actually come forward and decided to go ahead and file civil lawsuits against Mr. Epstein," Kuvin said "I was retained by not only that first victim, but also two other girls who were courageous enough to step forward and file a suit against Mr. Epstein."

"When the first cases were resolved, the young girls were extremely upset at the way that the US Attorney's Office handled that case," Kuvin explained." Really, they kind of felt revictimized by the system itself, by the US Attorney's office, because nobody seemed to care about them."

"I think that's why they really focused as much as they did, because they knew as attorneys on their behalf, we were fighting vigorously to get Mr. Epstein and to get admissions out of him and to conduct investigations. We were deposing under oath his house manager and the police chief and the lead investigator and his cook and his pilot and him. You know, the US Attorney's Office wasn't doing that. We were, on behalf of the victims."

Indeed, Epstein had been able to evade a trial, but it was in the civil cases that he had to answer tough questions for the very first time, leaving prison to sit for uncomfortable depositions that were recorded on tape.

"I took Mr. Epstein's deposition twice," Kuvin said. "On the first occasion that I took his deposition, as I walked in the room, he really attempted as best he could to maintain eye contact. He had a big grin on his face, always looked smug."

He continued:

> You got the feeling that he always felt as though he was the smartest man in the room but yet he always wanted to try to ingratiate himself and be friendly with everyone that was around.
>
> He had two lawyers protecting him during the deposition that I took. The first one, his criminal lawyer and his civil lawyer, they sat there objecting to questions constantly, while Mr. Epstein would just sit back and smirk. He'd look over to them during questioning if he was concerned whether he should assert his fifth amendment right or just go ahead and answer questions.
>
> He would periodically answer questions that he knew were insignificant, that he could talk about, like where he may have gone to school or where he grew up. While at the same time objecting to other questions that were basic such as "what's your address in Palm Beach" that he thought may be able to incriminate him.
>
> I asked him, in his first deposition, the most significant question right at the beginning: whether or not in fact his private parts were the shape of an egg? He smirked almost to the point of a laugh.
>
> His lawyers became indignant, and then he got up and walked out of a deposition. After that, I went to court and filed a motion for sanctions against him for walking out on me and the judge granted my motion for sanctions and awarded me $800 for the

time I spent having to go back and take a second deposition of him.

In the second deposition, I asked even more salacious questions of him which he never agreed to answer. Questions about sex toys that were found in his bedroom, massage oils found in his bedroom, women that he either knew, places he had gone, things he had done, sexual positions. And the goal of all that was to see if I could get him angry, or upset, or throw him off to where he would actually spurt something out that could incriminate him.

Having said that, during the entire time, all he would do is just smirk, smile, sit back in a very creepy way, and just read a prepared statement that his lawyers would give him regarding his Fifth Amendment.

After the whole thing was said and done, from both the first and the second deposition, I guess the best way to describe it is just creepy. This was a guy that when you got in a room with him, after you left the room, you felt like you needed to take a shower.

I met him a third occasion at a mediation where we resolved some of the cases together, and he was there along with his lawyers. And during that process he really took over and wanted to talk about how . . . Well, put it this way, he took over the discussions and not his lawyers. And he, I think, always felt as though he was the smartest man in the room even beyond his own legal team.

But even on that occasion, I can't recall ever reaching across the table and trying to shake the man's hand. Even though he was an adversary on the other side of the case, he always seemed to want to try to be friends with everyone. Saying, "How are you? How are you doing?" And, "Nice to meet you." And it was just as though he could not get out of that routine of trying to make everyone his friend.

Eventually, Kuvin's civil cases were settled and the victims involved got undisclosed payouts. The cash did not, however, buy their silence; they were free to discuss the case and the allegations at will moving forward. It was just the exact amount of their settlements that were kept quiet.

Kuvin explained, "On behalf of the victims, we wanted to protect the girls, frankly, because we didn't want friends or people outside of litigation knowing what type of money these young girls may have gotten from Mr. Epstein. Obviously, with money comes hangers-on and other people that may be involved in their life and property. So we kept the amounts confidential to protect the girls as much as anyone else. But the facts of those settlements, they were allowed to talk about to anyone they chose to talk to."

Bradley Edwards, another high-profile victims' attorney, later admitted in court documents that his three clients had received a total of $5.5 million in settlements.

Still, it wasn't entirely a happy ending for anyone involved. During the course of that litigation and the police investigation that had preceded it, Kuvin claims, Epstein's team had gone all out on the girls, with rough-and-tumble tactics designed to exploit their every weakness and perhaps intimidate them into silence, adding insult on top of the many psychological injuries they had already suffered.

"I was followed," one Epstein victim, who asked not to be identified, told these authors. "I received death threats on the phone. The life of my daughter was threatened, and at one point, a car tried to run me off the road. I am convinced Epstein was behind it all. He wanted to frighten me into not cooperating."

Kuvin recalled, "I can tell you that in representing the victims of Mr. Epstein, and going through some of the litigation, and seeing some of the hard-nosed tactics he had against my clients, having them followed by his private investigators, having black trucks drive up to their house and quickly drive away or sit outside their home, having his investigators interview people in their families, looking online at all of their backgrounds and information. As a lawyer on behalf of those clients, there were days where I definitely walked out to my car and I would remote start my car. Call it a hunch, call it a fear, call it just good practice. It was definitely something that concerned me."

"As far as the victims, I can tell you more so the parents than victims were very angry," he continued. "And as a parent myself, I can tell you that I would have had my own personal thoughts about what I would want to see happen to Mr. Epstein outside of the court system."

Indeed, court documents obtained by this investigation show that Epstein's attorneys trolled the victims' social media pages for "evidence" of impropriety that they then submitted in the case in order to impeach them as witnesses. For example. attorneys circled and starred innocuous posts by the young girls, posts that would later be used against them.

Victim Michelle Licata, who filed a civil suit against Epstein, told reporter Marjorie Hernandez that the experience was like psychological warfare.

> It was really weird. It was me going back and forth from where I lived to Florida and meetings psychologists. It was Jeffrey Epstein's psychologists and psychiatrists and therapists. They were asking me a lot of questions and then I had to go to my own therapists and my own psychologist.
>
> Then I had depositions on cameras with his lawyers and my lawyers. I felt it was like a cat-and-mouse game. Let's see how long we can keep her mind going while we figure out some kind of sweetheart deal.
>
> They were asking me questions about things that had happened in my life. They were talking to me about, "So you don't think that this was very traumatic in your life and that's probably why you're so 'screwed up'?" Pretty much, that's what they were saying. "These little things that happened in your life, you don't think that's the reason for why you are angry at the world?"
>
> That's when I got on to his lawyer about what he does. I was like, "If you think that what happened to me in my life compares

to anywhere near to what has happened with me and your client," I was like, "you're crazy." Making those two comparisons, no. *This* is why I'm messed up in my life. Stop talking to me about *those* things. They were trying to do exactly what Jeffrey Epstein did.

They were trying to go into your subconscious, into your mind and try and find your weak spots, and try and see what they could use against you in the court of law. These people were giving me thick books and packets of lawyer talk and I had to fill out these questions about "how many people have you slept with? Name every single person you've ever done anything with?"

I called up my lawyer. I was like, "Kissing or sex?" And she said they want to know every single person. I'm like, "And what does this word mean? What's a deposition?" I was still nineteen years old not knowing what was going on.

They went after just me. They were trying to make me look bad against myself, to try and make me feel like I wasn't credible. I was like, "No, I wasn't a hooker, and no I wasn't a stripper." I mean, I was in high school. I was friends with this girl that brought me there. I mean, what are you expecting to find? "When did you start sleeping with these guys?" I'm like, I mean do you want dates or what do you want from me? I don't know.

It was a nightmare. This whole process is a never-ending nightmare. I just wish that somebody would do something and shut it down and get it done and over with and let everybody have their lives back.

But the fight for justice was far from over. Almost immediately after Epstein's secret sweetheart deal was exposed, two victims filed a lawsuit against the US government itself.

Identified only as Jane Doe #1 and Jane Doe #2, the plaintiffs were two victims who claimed that the federal government had not notified them of

Epstein's plea deal—a violation of the Crime Victims Rights Act. That law, passed in 2004, grants all victims the right to prior notice of any court proceedings in their case, as well as the right to appear and speak at any hearing, as appropriate. In Epstein's case, neither right had been granted.

Perversely, the government at first tried to argue that the CVRA did not apply, because federal charges against Epstein had never been filed due to the very same plea deal they had covered up. The court firmly rejected that position.

Since the non-prosecution agreement at issue had prevented any future federal charges against Epstein, a judge ruled, the victims did have legal standing to coverage under CVRA. With that established, the judge deferred any judgment as to whether they were entitled to relief or damages until more evidence could be gathered.

At that time, in 2015, two more victims attempted to join the case: Jane Doe #3 and Jane Doe #4. This team broke the story: The new victims claimed that since their circumstances were so similar to the first two plaintiffs, adding them to the case would cause little delay. What's more, in new court documents, the two victims made even more explosive claims.

Jane Doe #3, later revealed to be Virginia Roberts Giuffre, took aim at Ghislaine Maxwell:

> In 1999, Jane Doe #3 was approached by Ghislaine Maxwell, one of the main women whom Epstein used to procure under-aged girls for sexual activities and a primary co-conspirator in his sexual abuse and sex trafficking scheme.
>
> In fact, it became known to the government that Maxwell herself regularly participated in Epstein's sexual exploitation of minors, including Jane Doe #3.
>
> Maxwell persuaded Jane Doe #3 (who was then fifteen years old) to come to Epstein's mansion in a fashion very similar to the manner in which Epstein and his other co-conspirators

coerced dozens of other children (including Jane Doe #1 and Jane Doe #2).

When Jane Doe #3 began giving Epstein a "massage," Epstein and Maxwell turned it into a sexual encounter, as they had done with many other victims.

Epstein then became enamored with Jane Doe #3, and with the assistance of Maxwell converted her into what is commonly referred to as a "sex slave." Epstein kept Jane Doe #3 as his sex slave from about 1999 through 2002, when she managed to escape to a foreign country and hide out from Epstein and his co-conspirators for years.

From 1999 through 2002, Epstein frequently sexually abused Jane Doe #3, not only in West Palm Beach, but also in New York, New Mexico, the US Virgin Islands, in international airspace on his Epstein's private planes, and elsewhere. Epstein also sexually trafficked the then-minor Jane Doe, making her available for sex to politically-connected and financially-powerful people. Epstein's purposes in "lending" Jane Doe (along with other young girls) to such powerful people were to ingratiate himself with them for business, personal, political, and financial gain, as well as to obtain potential blackmail information.

Filed in the last hours of 2014, the documents were incredibly explosive—and we rushed to parse them. Roberts clearly, emphatically, and unemotionally accused Epstein, Maxwell, and their coconspirators of doing the kinds of things that only had been whispered about for years.

At the time, police had not released files or videos to us, and we had few documents that described the horrors Epstein had committed in the victims' own words.

It was a new level of disturbing.

What's more, for the first time, Roberts unleashed on Prince Andrew:

Jane Doe #3 was forced to have sexual relations with this Prince when she was a minor in three separate geographical locations: in London (at Ghislaine Maxwell's apartment), in New York, and on Epstein's private island in the US Virgin Islands (in an orgy with numerous other under-aged girls).

Epstein instructed Jane Doe #3 that she was to give the Prince whatever he demanded and required Jane Doe #3 to report back to him on the details of the sexual abuse.

Maxwell facilitated Prince Andrew's acts of sexual abuse by acting as a "madame" for Epstein, thereby assisting in internationally trafficking Jane Doe #3 (and numerous other young girls) for sexual purposes.

"Epstein also trafficked Jane Doe #3 for sexual purposes to many other powerful men," the court filings claimed, "including numerous prominent American politicians, powerful business executives, foreign presidents, a well-known Prime Minister, and other world leaders. Epstein required Jane Doe #3 to describe the events that she had with these men so that he could potentially blackmail them."

Indeed, in the years after Epstein was released from prison, his information-gathering and blackmail system went into overdrive like never before. Despite the fact that he was a convicted sex felon, still facing lawsuits and allegations in Florida, the highest levels of society stood waiting to welcome him back from prison with open arms.

Epstein walked right into them.

CHAPTER 12

THE SMARTEST MEN IN THE WORLD

After Jeffrey Epstein's arrest and the subsequent flood of lawsuits, he was considered radioactive in the political realm. Bill Clinton and other bold names on D.C.'s Beltway and beyond insisted that they'd had no idea what Epstein was doing with the young girls around him; the implication being, now that they knew, they would never talk to him again.

However, one of the most prominent Lolita Express passengers didn't seem to mind being linked to and even photographed with a sex felon: Britain's Prince Andrew.

In what now seems like a catastrophic misstep that launched the most sensational scandal in Buckingham Palace history, Prince Andrew remained a public ally of the convicted pedophile even after his release from prison. The Prince was a guest of honor at Epstein's Manhattan "welcome home from prison" bash when he finished his sentence in 2010.

Organized by an old-school publicist, Peggy Siegal, the event had a star-studded guest list of New York's elite. Did they know exactly who was hosting the party?

Among those who joined Epstein and Andrew that night were news anchor Katie Couric, talk show host Charlie Rose, comedian Chelsea Handler, filmmaker Woody Allen, and President Clinton's former senior advisor, George Stephanopoulos.

Just a few months before, Siegal had organized another high-society event at the mansion: A Yom Kippur dinner for 120 people—including their children.

Despite Epstein's sex offender status, he and Prince Andrew seemed chummier than ever in 2010. They were photographed strolling together through Central Park during one visit, and Andrew was even caught on video poking his grinning face out Epstein's front door to say goodbye to a departing young brunette.

Following the release of that video, Buckingham Palace once again found itself having to issue another statement to "clarify the facts"—this time personally signed by Prince Andrew himself.

It read:

> At no stage during the limited time I spent with him did I see, witness or suspect any behaviour of the sort that subsequently led to his arrest and conviction. I have said previously that it was a mistake and an error to see him after his release in 2010 and I can only reiterate my regret that I was mistaken to think what I thought I knew of him was evidently not the real person, given what we now know. I have tremendous sympathy for all those affected by his actions and behaviour. This is a difficult time for everyone involved and I am at a loss to be able to understand or explain Mr. Epstein's lifestyle. I deplore the exploitation of any human being and would not condone, participate in, or encourage any such behaviour.

For Epstein, it was becoming clear that his time rubbing shoulders with lawmakers and royals was over. Luckily, there was an entirely new class of movers and shakers for him to exploit: brilliant scientists and tech gurus who were building the future—and could make his wildest dreams of ultimate power come true.

Epstein had already shown an interest in cultivating such circles.

In 2006, he hosted a conference at the Ritz-Carlton on St. Thomas, which attracted the likes of Stephen Hawking. During one night of the conference, guests were shuttled over to Little St. James for a barbecue and submarine tour. According to reports, the sub was custom-fitted for Hawking's wheelchair. A photo of the event shows him being personally attended to by a young blonde with her hair in a ponytail.

Unlike politicians, however, scientists seemed more willing to overlook his status as a heinous sex offender. Yet again, Ghislaine would pave the way.

In 2009, Epstein was still in prison when he began planning his grand return to the establishment. Ghislaine's sister, Isabel, was in a relationship with leading visual theorist Al Seckel, and he worked with Epstein to plan a triumphant 2010 scientific conference on St. Thomas and Little St. James.

Just three months after Epstein's prison release, Seckel granted him a long, discursive interview that was published on the front page of Epstein's new—and bizarre—science blog, JeffreyEpsteinScience.org.

On the blog, Epstein clearly defined his new, post-prison identity, carefully leaving out the bad bits.

Jeffrey E. Epstein serves as the Chairman and Chief Executive Officer of the Financial Trust Company. Mr. Epstein started his career at Bear Stearns with an educational background in physics. He has been a Trustee of the Institute Of International Education Inc. since October 2001.

He serves as a Director of Financial Trust Company. Previously, Mr. Epstein was a Member of the Trilateral Commission and the Council on Foreign Relations as well as the New York Academy of Science. He is also a former Rockefeller University Board Member. Currently, Mr. Epstein is actively involved in the Santa Fe Institute, the Theoretical Biology Initiative at the Institute for Advanced Study, the Quantum Gravity Program at the University of Pennsylvania, and also sits on the Mind, Brain & Behavior Advisory Committee at Harvard.

Jeffrey Epstein's philanthropic affiliations include The COUQ Foundation. He is a member of the Edge Group, an internationally respected group of thinkers and achievers.

Of course, he forgot to mention the one qualification that would define his life: he was a registered sex offender.

Refreshed and reinvigorated, Epstein entered his new milieu with a splash.

On November 6, 2010, Epstein and Seckel announced the "Mindshift" conference, which would be hosted and funded by Epstein, on St. Thomas and Little St. James.

They boasted of a star-studded guest list of science icons: Nobel Prize–winning physicist Murray Gell-Mann, bestselling author and theoretical physicist Leonard Mlodinow, MIT professor and artificial intelligence researcher Gerald Jay Sussman, neuroscientist Christof Koch, Nobel Laureate Frances Arnold, Silicon Valley wunderkind Paul Kirkaas, and more.

In the following weeks, Epstein posted interviews with more leading scientists on his new website. Then, in January, the Mindshift conference took place as advertised. Isabel Maxwell attended as Seckel's guest, along with the other notables.

Isabel's friend, Laura Goldman, said, "That was in 2010, after the 2008 charges. They obviously forgave him."

The same month as the conference, Seckel was listed on Epstein's website among the scientists supposedly funded by the pedophile.

But then something unexpected happened. In March 2011, Seckel and Isabel Maxwell were charged with fraud by a mysterious company called Ensign Consulting. Based in the US Virgin Islands—like so many of Epstein's businesses—Ensign claimed that Seckel had advised the company on investments, only to run off with more than $500,000 for himself.

Almost at the same time as the lawsuit became public, Seckel's interview with Epstein was removed from his science website. By the end of the month, the entire website was gone. Days after that, Seckel was in a terrifying car wreck that totaled his Lexus.

Suddenly, seemingly out of nowhere, Seckel issued a signed "declaration" in May 2011 clarifying his relationship with Epstein.

I have no personal knowledge of Epstein's private life. Mr. Epstein has not discussed his private life with me and our discussions have been strictly limited to intellectual or philanthropic subjects. . . .

I have never met nor had any discussions with any woman or girl who was under the age of 18 (or previously underaged) who I know to have had intimate or non-intimate contact with Mr. Epstein. . . .

I understand that there has been a subpoena issued to depose me based on alleged 'credible' information that I have been in the presence of Mr. Epstein and women or girls under the age of 18. I have not. Nor have I witnessed any sexual behavior or even innuendo by Mr. Epstein. . . .

I further understand that I have been identified as having been in Mr. Epstein's presence at the same time as famous or "high-profile" people were present. Other than those in the scientific community, I am unaware of any persons in our mutual presence who could be described this way."

Was there truly an ongoing investigation into Epstein at that time? None ever became public.

More importantly, just who was Al Seckel protecting with that decree? Himself? The answer is not immediately clear.

What is certain, however, is that from there, Seckel's life took a dramatic turn for the worse. Hounded by the Ensign lawsuit, he and Isabel—now his wife—filed for bankruptcy and fled to France. More messy lawsuits and humiliation followed.

Then in spring 2015, Seckel went hiking in France and vanished.

A massive search ensued, with participants even including those who had attended his conference with Epstein. By June 2015, Seckel's rental car was found at the side of a cliff. About a month later, his body reportedly was found at the bottom of that same cliff. The cause of death was unclear. Some reports claimed that like Robert Maxwell, who fell from his yacht and drowned, Seckel's unfortunate end had been precipitated by a "heart attack."

A few weeks later, *Tablet* magazine published an explosive article—written when he was alive—that claimed Seckel had cultivated information-gathering relationships with powerful people in the worlds of science, politics, media, and more. What's more, the article claimed that Seckel had been actively trying to sell the correspondence and personal files of his father-in-law, Robert Maxwell, a businessman and Mossad spy, in the weeks before his death. Did he take them from Epstein and Ghislaine? In 2004, this team found, Epstein was holding such documents at his Palm Beach home, years before meeting Seckel.

In any case, he'd be found dead before he found a buyer.

***

Despite the tech luminaries who visited Little St. James, it was never really the hub of Epstein's scientific pursuits. Instead, Epstein cultivated scientific connections at his 10,000-acre Zorro Ranch, outside of Santa Fe, New Mexico.

In 2010, Epstein donated $25,000 to the nearby Santa Fe Institute, devoted to "the big questions" about science. Already, he was insinuating his way into his new crowd. Over the years, he would donate a quarter of a million dollars to the facility, claiming on his website that he was "actively involved" in the Institute, presumably by way of his donations. The Institute would later insist they had no idea about his background.

In some sense, though, Epstein made Zorro Ranch an institute of his own.

"Our important people were mostly scientists," Deidre Stratton, the woman tasked with recruiting young massage therapists for Epstein in New Mexico, told *Epstein: Dead Men Tell No Tales.* "Jeffrey helped back their research."

Stratton continued:

> He would often have . . . you know, like the guy that won the
> Nobel Prize for discovering the quark in quantum physics.

Epstein's private island, Little St. James, was the setting for some of his most disturbing assaults, victims claimed. (The Mega Agency)

Epstein's gaudy study at his New York City mansion was exposed in the July 2019 police raid. (The Mega Agency)

Police used a crowbar to break down the door to Epstein's NY mansion, which was secured by a high-power deadbolt used by the Department of Defense. (The Mega Agency)

Epstein and Prince Andrew were photographed together in Central Park in 2010, shortly after his prison stint. The prince now claims that he made the trip to end their friendship. (The Mega Agency)

Epstein's NY study featured a stuffed tiger. Nearby was a taxidermied poodle. (The Mega Agency)

During the police raid on Epstein's NY home, passerby noticed this painting of Bill Clinton in the Oval Office wearing a blue dress. A nod to Monica? (The Mega Agency)

Epstein's New York home was built around an imposing entrance. (The Mega Agency)

Virginia Roberts at Zorro Ranch in New Mexico. (Palm Beach County State Attorney's Office)

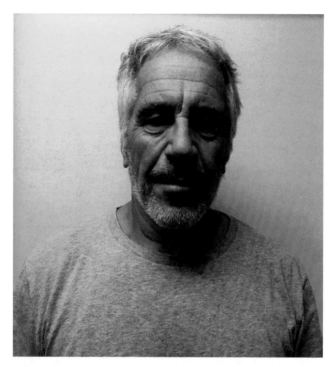

Epstein's grim July 2019 mugshot showed how far he had fallen. (The Mega Agency)

In this photo of Ghislaine Maxwell that surfaced after Epstein's arrest, she was seen wearing a pinkie ring nearly identical to one worn in the past by Epstein. Was it a sign? (The Mega Agency)

A guy that won the Nobel Prize for a DNA discovery, people that help to found Microsoft. Those were the kind of people that were there.

Scientific and brilliant. They would have very erudite conversations over meals. You would pick up a word here and there. Obviously, you couldn't really hear the whole thing.

They would invite them to lunch and Ghislaine would have this tablet and she would write down the facts that they would tell them. At one point she told me, "Well, you get the information from an expert and then you get rid of them."

Like Epstein's other properties, Zorro Ranch was both over the top and disturbing in the details.

Ean Royal lived with his ranch-hand father on the property in the years after Epstein's Florida prison stint.

"It was super lavish," Royal said.

He continued:

There was an observatory room that had a telescope. Loads of books. Like a little study, it had a balcony and you could look out through this telescope and kind of look wherever because you had an open sight. This was on the second floor.

There was this huge parlor room. Almost looked like something you'd find in Sherlock Holmes. You'd walk in there. There was this really nice brown desk on one side. You got couches in the middle, and then you got loads of books everywhere. Of course books were all over. It's totally like a Gatsby thing. All for show. It really looked like there could've been a secret room. Like if I pulled one of the books, the shelf would move over or something.

It was mind-blowing. Like, he had a freaking stuffed sheep in the elevator. I would get into the elevator, and you'd be just standing next to this stuffed animal. Like taxidermy. A straight taxidermy animal. Not like a fake. Just in the elevator. Just chilling.

Beautiful furniture. And it just didn't make sense. Because it's like, "Man, you have all of this stuff, and no one even uses it. This house is empty 80 percent of the time, and we just come in to maintenance it. We just check it out." I had that conversation with my dad a lot. I was like, "Why is this here if he doesn't even use it?' You have all this vacation ranch and land, and you don't even use it? That's insane."

Even stranger is the fact that hat to this day, the FBI has not raided the property; at least, according to public reports and local witnesses.

"It's very weird to me that they haven't, because there's a vacation ranch out in the middle of freaking nowhere. Like literally nowhere. Like on acres of ranch," Royal said.

"Acres of land. Why wouldn't they check it?"

He added:

Especially when they have the multimillion-dollar mansion, and then basically a tiny little town at the base of the ranch with all of these different housings for people to live in, and then housings for vehicles, and then all of the animals there. The front of it is a vacation ranch.

But, why would it just be a vacation ranch? When I was younger, I was always kind of curious. It was like, "So he's spending all of this money just to run a vacation ranch that he doesn't even come to?" I'm like, "He has all of these animals, and all of these people that just maintain the ranch." And it seems like the whole point of it was to just bring people there for some reason, whatever it may be, to be entertained.

Because if he had guests over, like I said, the guests would have entertainment. They would go shooting, they would go horse-back riding. But as far as anything outside of that, they couldn't have just been going to do that. You know what I mean?

They wouldn't just go to the ranch to shoot some guns and ride horses. Especially if they're important people. I'm sure what would happen is Epstein was buttering them up, and giving them this as a gift, and then trying to get something out of them or from them, or whatever it may be. Basically, buttering them up before he pitches whatever ideas, or thoughts he might have to do with whatever, which is why governors would end up being there. Politician would end up being there.

According to Stratton, the ranch did feature unique entertainment for its guests.

"I'll tell you one thing that happened, like every time practically," Stratton said.

"They had a goat that looked like Merlin, long horns, long hair. It was obviously a male goat, if you know anything about goats.

"Anyway, so they had this little game where they would have the girls or a girl, whomever, they were entertaining down to the stables and the stable lady named Shanna, she would already be sitting on a stool milking the goat. It was staged.

"She he had this little jar with a little milk in it. So then the next thing they would say is, 'Would you like to try to milk the goat?' So of course, the girl sat on the stool and Shanna would reach her hands under there to his like 'udder,' which was actually his sexual organs and tried to milk him.

"Well, nothing would happen. Then suddenly they'd go, 'Oh, it's a male goat!'

"That poor goat. I started feeling badly for the goat."

***

Epstein's employees were required to keep quiet about what they saw and heard on the ranch.

Nancy Sowle, owner of the local general store, told us that the air of secrecy surrounding the ranch was unmistakable—and oppressive.

"Everything was so secretive up there," Sowle said. "The employees had to sign that they would never disclose any information. It was just all very secretive, and as you found out, you can't get past the gate and what have you. It bothers me that there are people like that, obviously, but I guess based on everything else that we've heard about Epstein and all of these other locations, it's upsetting. But it's not surprising, also, that it occurred out here.

"I don't know," Sowle continued. "I think maybe people move out here because they think that we're so far away from the media and other things, so maybe that's why he decided to build up here."

Ean Royal remembered: "My dad was super secretive about it, of course, because he was told that was his job. It's like, 'Don't say anything. Don't say his name.' All of this stuff.

"I would ask my dad and he was like, 'I can't tell you. I can't tell you his name.' Then I think at one point he could tell me his first name. So, I learned Jeffrey is *Jeffrey.*

"I didn't have any personal connection with Jeffrey, but from what I understand, and how secretive everything was, like if there was a man that had nothing to hide, why was he hiding everything? You know what I mean? I would definitely say that he's a monster. He was hiding stuff. He was doing a lot of stuff with a lot of important people. But if he's talking to politicians and people who are in power and actually interacting with them and bringing them to his ranch, he's got an evil M.O. [modus operandi]."

Epstein's ultimate goal was—if not evil—certainly unusual. In the early 2000s, he made it clear to several close friends that he had embraced transhumanism, the belief that science and technology would eventually allow humans to evolve beyond the confines of the body.

Indeed, as he said before prison, "Your body can be contained. But not your mind."

In pursuing that goal, he hoped to use Zorro Ranch as his testing ground.

We have independently corroborated through sources that Epstein planned to deep-freeze his body—specifically his head and penis—so that he could be thawed in the future, supposedly when science had advanced enough for reanimation.

Another aspect of his master plan allegedly included impregnating dozens of women to strengthen the Earth's gene pool—with his own genes. Scientist Jaron Lanier, who once overheard Epstein prattle on at a dinner party, said Epstein had "based his idea for a baby ranch on accounts of the Repository for Germinal Choice, which was to be stocked with the sperm of Nobel laureates." (Originally named the Hermann J. Muller Repository for Germinal Choice, the Repository was a sperm bank that operated in Escondido, Calif., from 1980 to 1999. The Repository was commonly believed to have accepted only donations from recipients of the Nobel Prize, although it did accept donations from non-Nobelists, also.)

Of course, Epstein's big idea was nothing new. The Nazis had called it eugenics.

To Epstein's former attorney Alan Dershowitz, such talk was commonplace with Epstein, if seriously disturbing. "At one point, at a meeting, he talked about something that sounded too eugenics for most of us," Dershowitz told our reporter.

"There was a lot of [talk] about how eugenics had been misused in the 1930s, and none of us wanted to have anything to do with anything that sounded eugenic."

According to Dershowitz, "Mostly he was interested in evolutionary biology that didn't relate to human beings, related to what Darwin had done and others had done. That's why he was particularly interested in Stephen Jay Gould." (Gould died in 2002, long before Epstein's crimes became public.)

"But he never ever discussed with anybody I know, any of those weird ideas."

Had he, Dershowitz claimed: "He would have been laughed out of Harvard."

Perhaps that is why he kept such discussions to carefully selected companions at his New Mexico enclave. To Epstein, acceptance by academics—and by Harvard, most of all—was paramount.

Epstein's former friend Jesse Kornbluth explained the obsession: "I went to Harvard, and Harvard was extremely meaningful for Jeffrey.

"If you look at pictures of him in later life, he's wearing a Harvard sweatshirt, he's giving money to Harvard. He owns an office in Harvard Square, and is palling around with Harvard scientists. Harvard was the kind of validation he sought, and it was validation which I had already acquired."

As with most things he wanted, Epstein tried first to buy his way into Harvard. University President Lawrence S. Bacow sent an email to students and alumni almost exactly one month after Epstein's death that laid bare the extent of his contributions:

Our review to date indicates that between 1998 and 2007, Epstein made a number of gifts to support various faculty and institutional research activities across the University. The largest of these was a $6.5 million gift in 2003 to support the Program for Evolutionary Dynamics.

The University received other gifts, which totaled approximately $2.4 million, based on current information. Each of these gifts from Epstein and his affiliated foundations to Harvard University predates his guilty plea in June 2008. To date, we have uncovered no gifts received from Epstein or his foundation following his guilty plea.

Moreover, we specifically rejected a gift from Epstein following his conviction in 2008. We have also recently learned that Stephen Kosslyn, a former faculty member and a beneficiary of Epstein's philanthropy, designated Epstein as a Visiting Fellow in the Department of Psychology in 2005. We are seeking to learn more about the nature of that appointment from Dr. Kosslyn, who no longer works at the University.

Epstein's cash bought him respect on campus. In June 2003, a writer for *The Crimson* penned a fawning article about Epstein's contributions. (Oddly, it would be that freshman author's last contribution to the paper.)

Noting that Epstein "donated $30 million this year to Harvard for the founding of a mathematical biology and evolutionary dynamics program," the article boasted of his "bevy of eminent friends that includes princes, presidents and Nobel Prize winners." One such colleague was then-President of Harvard, Lawrence "Larry" Summers: "The two serve together on the Trilateral Commission and the Council on Foreign Relations, two elite international relations organizations," the article explained.

Separately, Epstein also was a top donor for Harvard's Hasty Pudding theater troupe as late as 2018. (The group announced in October 2019 that they would be donating to an anti-sex-trafficking nonprofit following the revelation.)

The nature of Epstein's role as Visiting Fellow remains murky. He did, however, use his time and vaunted placement at Harvard to cultivate even more important friendships.

One of the leaders of the psychology department in the time that Epstein was there was Stephen Pinker. Popular among students, Pinker was known for his cloud of curly white hair and bestselling books, such as *The Language Instinct* and *How the Mind Works*.

In 2007, when Epstein was facing monstrous allegations in Florida, Pinker contributed his professional opinion to a disturbing legal document in the case, one that argued Epstein was *not guilty* of using the Internet to lure teen victims. Actually, the document implied, any luring had been done in person.

Pinker has said that being categorized as a friend or even coconspirator of Epstein is seriously misguided. In a statement, he called it an "annoying irony" that his association with Epstein would be a black mark on his record, since "I could never stand the guy, never took research funding from him and always tried to keep my distance."

As with most statements of denial regarding Epstein, that last sentence raises an eyebrow. Pinker appears in the flight logs for the "Lolita Express" in 2002, long before Epstein got his official position at Harvard. Even more disturbingly, he was photographed lunching and chatting with Epstein at a 2014 lunch—more than five years after he became a convicted sex felon.

Pinker explained away the chilling photo on the social media site Twitter: "I have no relationship with Epstein & have taken no funding from him. Our circles have occasionally overlapped: In 02, my lit agent invited me to join a group of east-coast TED speakers Epstein flew to CA. In 14, Krauss seated me next to him at a lunch, & someone snapped a photo."

But the very next year, Pinker tweeted a link to a legal argument from the defense in Virginia Roberts Giuffre's civil lawsuit—a document that refuted her claims.

So far, the scandal has only managed to subject Pinker to hundreds of angry tweets and dozens of probing blog posts.

As for Pinker and Epstein's pal Lawrence Krauss, who also appeared in the 2014 lunch photo, he has not emerged unscathed.

There is more of a paper trail connecting Krauss to Epstein than the one that smeared Pinker's reputation. Voice messages to Epstein from Krauss obtained by this team show several calls from the scientist to Epstein's Palm Beach home.

One, sent on January 7, 2004, read, "Thank you for the evening last night in NYC." Epstein's secretary wrote, "You can call him about time and money."

Just over a year later, on February 28, 2005: "He has sent you some faxes that he would like to follow up."

Later than that message, but undated: "He had meeting with filmmaker and he sympathize [sic] with project."

In 2018, Krauss left his post at Arizona State University amid a cloud of scandal—actually, one that had very little to do with Epstein.

The theoretical physicist and astrophysicist faced an onslaught of sexual misconduct claims at the height of the #MeToo movement. In just one disturbing example of the allegations, a woman claimed he had grabbed her breasts at a ritzy conference gala. Dr. Krauss denied the claims: "To be clear, I have never harassed or assaulted anyone and have most certainly not exhibited gender discrimination in my professional dealings at the university or elsewhere."

Down the road from Harvard, at MIT, Epstein's contributions were even cloudier. In September 2019, Joichi Ito stepped down from MIT's Media Lab after the *New Yorker* reported he had tried to cover up donations from Epstein.

A convicted child molester, Epstein was actually on MIT's list of "disqualified" donors following his prison stint. Ito took his money anyways, the *New Yorker* reported, camouflaging nearly $2 million in donations.

Ito was shameless in his greed. In one email, he wrote of an Epstein donation: "Make sure this gets reported as anonymous."

Epstein also channeled funds from his famous friends like Bill Gates to the lab. In another email, the lab's then–director of development and strategy, Peter Cohen, wrote, "This is a $2M gift from Bill Gates directed by Jeffrey Epstein. For gift recording purposes, we will not be mentioning Jeffrey's name as the impetus for this gift." (Gates's rep denied Epstein had anything to do with the donation.)

What did these men get from their associations with Epstein? Beyond the thrill of flying high on private jet flights and secluded Caribbean islands, the appeal was obvious: Epstein donated millions in grants and gifts through his many "foundations" each year, and advertised that fact on the front page of JeffreyEpsteinScience.com.

The company of beautiful young women, of course, would have been an added bonus.

For Epstein, the value of these men was not just in the way it made him—a college dropout—seem like a legitimate intellectual leader by association. The discoveries and research of these men could have had serious applications in the worlds of armament, technology, and surveillance.

In short, their lunchtime chitchat became Epstein's offerings to the international intelligence community.

CHAPTER 13

CAUGHT

By early 2019, it seemed that the world had forgotten about Jeffrey Epstein and his crimes. To him, it may have seemed—at last—that he'd gotten away with it all.

The civil cases in Florida were moving slowly through the justice system. In December 2018, he paid to settle a lawsuit with victim attorney Bradley Edwards, preventing any trial and silencing his victims yet again. Several women had been ready to take the stand, but they were pushed yet again into the shadows of silence.

More than ten years after Jane Does #1 and 2 had filed their lawsuit against the US government regarding Epstein's non-prosecution agreement, that too had yet to bear legal any fruit. But by February 2019, that all changed.

On February 7, 2019, the Department of Justice confirmed that they had begun an investigation into whether there had been "professional misconduct" in the unusual handling of Epstein's secret plea deal.

Two weeks later, US District Judge Kenneth A. Marra ruled in favor of Jane Does #1 and 2 in Florida, agreeing that the United States government had indeed broken the law during their handling of the nonprosecution agreement.

"Particularly problematic was the government's decision to conceal the existence of the [nonprosecution agreement] and mislead the victims to believe that federal prosecution was still a possibility," Marra wrote, referring to one communication that told the plaintiffs to remain "patient."

"When the government gives information to victims, it cannot be misleading."

He continued:

> Epstein and his co-conspirators knowingly traveled in interstate and international commerce to sexually abuse Jane Doe 1, Jane Doe 2 and others, they committed violations of not only Florida law, but also federal law.
>
> In addition to his own sexual abuse of the victims, Epstein directed other persons to abuse the girls sexually. . . . Epstein worked in concert with others to obtain minors not only for his own sexual gratification, but also for the sexual gratification of others.

The net was closing in.

***

Flying on a private jet from Paris, landing at a private airport, skipping the baggage claim to head straight to the luxury ride awaiting—it was the only way to travel for someone of Jeffrey Epstein's milieu. For Jeffrey Epstein, July 6, 2019, had promised to be yet another serene and sumptuous evening in the life of a billionaire.

As the plane taxied down the tarmac, however, the sun setting on the horizon, he likely realized that there was going to be a change of plans. Epstein's bubble of wealth and privilege was popped, perhaps once and for all. Federal agents stood ready on the tarmac, swooping in to handcuff and arrest him as soon as he walked off the infamous "Lolita Express" for the very last time.

At the same time, federal agents swarmed his Manhattan palace, ready to open every drawer and search the rooms where visitors had never set foot. A crowbar got them through his massive solid oak front doors, as onlookers watched, shocked.

To no one's surprise, authorities found ample evidence to confirm that Epstein was trafficking girls for sex. In his safe, they discovered hundreds of sickening nude pictures of young victims, and the graphic photographs matched the most disturbing details that Epstein's victims had provided.

He also had curated an organized library of digital videos that identified the names of his "friends" and the young girls they had violated. Federal agents seized all of it. They also recovered heaps of cash and diamonds, and a fake expired passport with Epstein's picture plastered inside. It listed his residence as Saudi Arabia. (In court, Epstein's lawyers argued that he'd never used the phony passport, but the document itself indicated that it'd been used to get into the United Kingdom, France, Spain, and Saudi Arabia. Epstein's attorneys said in a filing submitted to court that he obtained the passport because he felt it could give him some protection if he fell victim to an airline hijacking or a terrorist incident, and that it'd been expired for more than three decades.)

Importantly, the trove of evidence was not just proof of Epstein's sex crimes; the materials also corroborated the victims' claims that Epstein secretly recorded them in the act. Epstein and his coconspirators seemed poised for certain doom, as a copy of the voluminous evidence list was turned over to US District Judge Richard Berman.

Two days later, the US Attorney's Office for the Southern District of New York hosted a joint press conference with the Federal Bureau of Investigation. Entering the room, reporters were greeted with a massive blown-up photo of Epstein, and a phone number imploring potential victims to call the authorities.

Manhattan US Attorney Geoffrey S. Berman—an appointee of President Donald J. Trump—approached the podium to deliver the jaw-dropping news: *Jeffrey Epstein had been indicted for sex trafficking.* It was a day that had seemed like it would never come. For those of us who'd covered the case for years, and certainly for the victims, it had a surreal quality. Did we dare hope for justice this time around?

Berman began to speak:

Today, we announce the unsealing of sex trafficking charges against Jeffrey Epstein. The charges allege that Epstein sexually abused young girls by enticing them to engage in sex acts for money.

Epstein was arrested this past Saturday evening at Teterboro Airport aboard his private jet that had just landed from Paris, France. Epstein was taken to the Metropolitan Correctional Center in Manhattan.

And later today he will be presented before a Magistrate Judge Pitman and later a conference before District Court Judge Berman.

The United States attorney's office will take the position at that presentment and that conference that Epstein should be detained pending trial. Epstein is charged in a two-count indictment. First conspiracy to commit sex trafficking and second the substantive crime of sex trafficking of underage girls.

Beginning in at least 2002 and continuing until 2005, Epstein is alleged to have abused dozens of victims by causing them to engage in sex acts with him at his mansion in New York and at his estate in Palm Beach, Florida.

The victims, all underage girls at the time of the alleged conduct, were given hundreds of dollars in cash after each encounter either by Epstein or by one of Epstein's employees. The underage girls were initially recruited to provide Epstein with massages and often did so nude or partially nude.

These massages became increasingly sexual in nature and would typically include one or more sex acts as specified in the indictment. As alleged, Epstein also paid certain victims to recruit additional girls to be similarly abused. This allowed Epstein to create an ever-expanding web of new victims.

This conduct, as alleged, went on for years and it involved dozens of young girls, some as young as 14 years old at the time that they were allegedly abused. As alleged, Epstein was well aware that many of his victims were minors. And not surprisingly, many of the underage girls that Epstein allegedly victimized were particularly vulnerable to exploitation.

The alleged behavior shocks the conscience. And while the charged conduct is from a number of years ago, it is still profoundly important to the many alleged victims now young women. They deserve their day in court and we are proud to be standing up for them by bringing this indictment.

Combating sex trafficking and exploitation of children is a priority for this office and for the Department of Justice as the sexual abuse of a minor can have devastating effects on victims often lasting for years. That is why my office will not rest until the perpetrators of these types of crimes are brought to justice.

Victims' voices, including the many voices of Epstein's alleged victims must be heard. To that end I want to say to anyone who was watching this or hearing about our prosecution, if you believe you are a victim of this man Jeffrey Epstein. Or you have evidence or information leading to the conduct alleged in the indictment unsealed today, we want to hear from you. Please call. 1-800-CALL FBI, that's 1-800-CALL FBI.

The charges unsealed today reflect the hard work not only of this office, but by our law enforcement partners at the Federal Bureau of Investigation.

The FBI had failed to bring Epstein to justice back in Florida. Why should his victims believe that it would play out differently this time around, in another jurisdiction? William Sweeney, Assistant-Director-in-Charge of

the New York office of the FBI, stepped forward with a message. He
began:

> Preserving the innocence in children is one of the most import-
> ant responsibilities we carry as adults. Purposely failing children
> in any way is not an option.
>
> And yet there are some in society who have chosen to blatantly
> disregard this responsibility, using whatever means they have at
> their disposal to lure children into a life which they should never
> have been exposed. As we allege today, Jeffrey Epstein is one of
> those people.
>
> At approximately 5:30 p.m. on Saturday evening we arrested
> him at Teterboro Airport without incident. Epstein has been
> charged with one count each of sex trafficking and sex traffick-
> ing conspiracy.
>
> For at least a four-year period, covering the entirety of 2002
> through 2005, he is alleged to have sexually exploited and abused
> dozens of minor girls at his homes in New York City and in Palm
> Beach, Florida.
>
> The girls were recruited in a variety of ways, usually by employ-
> ees of Epstein and sometimes by fellow victims. The victims typ-
> ically received hundreds of dollars in cash. The estimated dozens
> of victims were as young as fourteen years old at the time of
> recruitment.
>
> Children who provided up steam massages while they were
> nude or partially nude. Children who were asked to engage in
> direct and indirect sex acts for money. Children who were enticed
> to do all these things at the hands of a man more than or nearly
> three times their age. Those who had been victimized by child
> sexual predators are frequently haunted by memories of these
> crimes well into their adulthood, often for the rest of their lives.
> They bear the burden of someone else's criminal behavior.

Too often, adults in our society have turned a blind eye to this type of criminal behavior alleged here. We have seen the excuses. The ignorance of many who didn't even bother to understand that this behavior is this persistent scourge against our society's vulnerable youth. And the willful blindness as to who the real villains are in this type of outrageous crime.

The villains are the adult perpetrators, not the children. Victims of child sex trafficking come from all walks of life. They are our neighbors, our students, young adults looking for help, vulnerable foster children, the list goes on and on and on.

To the victims who may be listening or get word of today's charges, the team standing here before you represents FBI Special Agents, NYPD detectives, analyst, victim specialist, prosecutors who make it their mission to listen to every individual who's been exploited and to advocate for the most vulnerable among us.

We are parents, we are community members, we are human beings. But as an FBI Special Agent and the head of this office, I have the privilege to represent and stand among many who make it our mission to put predators behind bars where they belong, regardless of the predator's power wealth or perceived connections.

Today, I'm asking everyone to take a good look at this man. If you have been victimized in any way or if you are somebody who has any additional information about his alleged illegal behavior, we want to hear from you. Whatever age you are now, whatever age you were then, no matter where or when the incident or incidents took place. . . .

Your bravery might just empower others to speak out about crimes committed against them. It's important to remember there never was nor will there be an excuse for this kind of behavior. We know that reliving these events can be brutal. We are here

to work side by side with you as you go through this process. You
should know that in the eyes of the FBI you come first.

Then, Berman jumped in again: "We're going to take some questions. But first
let me preface it by saying that there's been a lot of speculation in the media
about individuals affiliated or associated with defending Jeffrey Epstein."

"As you know, Justice Department guidelines prohibit us from talking
about such individuals, and so I just want to let you know that if that question comes up about any individual, my answer will be, no comment. And
that will be across the board no comment." That part of the investigation,
regarding the coconspirators, was clearly ongoing.

The first question raised by reporters was: If Epstein was bound by the
notorious Florida nonprosecution agreement, how had prosecutors been
able to bring new charges?

Berman explained, "Jeffrey Epstein entered into a non-prosecution
agreement with the Southern District of Florida. That agreement only
binds—by its terms only binds to Southern District of Florida. The Southern
District of New York is not bound by that agreement and is not a signatory
to that agreement."

The same would be true for his coconspirators.

***

Meanwhile, Epstein had a lot of time to consider his next move as he sat
locked up in a eight-by-eight jail cell. Immediately after his arrest, Epstein
had been taken directly to the Metropolitan Correctional Center, a
rust-colored federal detention facility in the heart of Lower Manhattan.

The "MCC" is where New York's most cold-blooded criminals are incarcerated while awaiting trial or bail. At the time, the MCC was the temporary
home of Mexican kingpin Joaquín "El Chapo" Guzmán and Trump's presidential campaign chairman Paul Manafort. Previous inmates included mob
boss John Gotti, financial fraudster Bernie Madoff, and the 1993 World
Trade Center bomber Ramzi Yousef.

In other words, it was secure. *Or so people thought.*

Located a few blocks from the Brooklyn Bridge and bustling Chinatown, MCC is one of several federal buildings in the immediate area. The US Attorney's office, NYPD headquarters, and City Hall are directly nearby. It is, in essence, meant to be the most secure area of the Big Apple.

Like each of the other eight hundred felons at MCC, Epstein was booked, stripped of his identity, and given his inmate number: 76318–054. He was taken to the ninth floor (also known as 9-South), which is a special housing unit for violent inmates and new arrivals who require protective custody. Epstein had to be kept out of the general population, it was thought, because every felon would hit him up—or rough him up—for money.

But segregation came at a price.

In 9-South, all 120 inmates are divided into sixty two-man cells. Epstein was locked up in cell number 123 with fifty-two-year-old Nicholas Tartaglione, a brawny retired policeman charged with executing four men in upstate New York.

The cells in 9-South don't have bars. Each eight-by-eight-foot unit is completely sealed off by a solid door, which has a narrow rectangular window and a "trap" where food trays are placed. The slot is also used to cuff inmates behind their back before the cell door is opened. Besides a bunk bed and a prominent toilet, each cell has a sink, a small shower in the corner, and a fixed desk and stool. A single frosted-glass window gave Epstein a few inches of daylight from the outside world.

Inmates are locked up for twenty-three-and-a-half hours a day. For the remaining thirty minutes, they are permitted to walk around a small portion of the tier: In Epstein's case, it was the "M-Tier." But according to an inmate who was in 9-South with Epstein, the 9-South guards "never let you out of the cell."

"It's a nightmare," the inmate told our investigator. "It's a hellhole for all of us. There are roaches and rats and it's never cleaned. The cell is rancid and they wouldn't give Epstein anything to clean it. . . . That place is out of control."

Two days after his arrest, on July 8, Epstein was let out of his cell to attend his first court hearing, where he was officially charged with sex trafficking and conspiracy to traffic minors for sex.

Not surprisingly, an arrogant Epstein pleaded not guilty. The judge scheduled his bail hearing for July 12.

Until then, Epstein and his attorneys planned to use every waking moment to plot their strategy.

"Epstein was taking over one of the only two rooms to meet lawyers in," his jailmate recalled. "He always tied up the lawyer's meeting room because he never wanted to be in that cell. That pissed off the inmates and the guards because it seemed like special treatment."

Worse, other witnesses claimed that Epstein and his lawyers routinely sat there in silence. His legal team, it seemed, was only there so he could stretch his legs outside the confines of his cell.

To further insulate himself from the harsh realities of prison, Epstein had his lawyers transfer money to the commissary accounts of several other inmates, one jail insider told these authors. The recipients could then use the "store credit" to purchase perks like toiletries, snacks, and stationery.

Social chameleon Epstein was at it again in an entirely new crowd, using his money to get people in his pocket.

But prison was not like his private island. When Epstein started throwing money around, it had an unintended consequence—one that may have proved deadly.

"The guards hated that Epstein got special treatment because of his money," his former jailmate told us exclusively. "The guards treated Epstein worse than any other inmate."

Inmates had to call the guards if they needed more toilet paper or cleaning supplies, for example, but the guards specifically ignored Epstein and made him "wait for everything," the jailhouse source claimed.

"They would never bring it when Epstein asked," his jailmate claimed. "They would always come if Epstein's bunkie (bunkmate) asked for anything, but never if he did. They would always say the guard on the next shift would take care of it, then that guard would say he knew nothing about it."

In his hasty attempt to win over his new peers, far from the glitz, glamor—and freedom—of life past, Epstein had irreversibly alienated the true prison power players.

The day after his first court hearing, Epstein and his victims got an unexpected surprise. Facing heavy criticism for his handling of Epstein's 2008 case, former Miami prosecutor Alexander Acosta resigned from Trump's cabinet under enormous pressure. Pressure, perhaps, for a public whipping boy to take the fall.

"I thought the right thing was to step aside," Acosta said, claiming that his continued presence as head of the United States Department of Labor would jeopardize President Trump's goal of "putting the American people first."

"This was him, not me," Trump declared. "I said, 'You don't have to do this.'"

Still, one might wonder if Trump was relieved to dissolve one of the conspicuous links between him and America's most famous pedophile, dating back decades—decades the public did not know about until this book.

Acosta stepped down and announced that he would devote his time to helping Epstein's rapidly expanding list of victims. At the time of this writing, it's unclear what form that mission will take, if any.

Back at MCC, however, Epstein and his legal team plotted their next move. Shockingly, it seemed they truly believed he was going to make bail. Epstein could have begun to daydream about a return to his mansion, with around the clock chaperones in tow, and an ankle bracelet to keep track of his every move.

At the bail hearing on July 12, the shape of their argument emerged.

Epstein's attorney focused on the fact that all of the New York accusations against him were alleged to have taken place before 2005. The next fourteen years, free of any public claims, supposedly proved Epstein's first jail term had "worked."

"He wasn't a predator that couldn't control his conduct," Martin Weinberg told the judge. "He disciplined himself."

The attorney argued that Epstein was not a "future danger" to girls and could be trusted in the real world.

"It's not like he's an out-of-control rapist," counsel insisted.

But Judge Berman was not convinced.

"How do you know that?" the Judge pressed, clearly skeptical that the "passage of time" was the proper way to measure the danger of having Epstein on the loose.

Assistant US Attorney Alex Rossmiller seized on that line of thinking.

"They concede that he has to discipline himself," the attorney answered. "This idea that he has 'disciplined himself' is a concession that he has an appetite for children."

In a Hail Mary play, Weinberg suggested setting Epstein's bail at $100 million—or more. But Rossmiller's determination to keep Epstein captive was unshakable.

"What the defendant is asking for here is special treatment, to build his own jail, to be limited in his own gilded cage," the defense attorney continued. "A person who needs these conditions should be detained. . . . He has every incentive to flee if he is released."

Judge Berman already knew all about *the talented Mr. Epstein.* He had been briefed on the pictures, the videos, the money, and the fake passport in Epstein's safe. He was aware of Epstein's habit of "generosity" to those who could help him get his way.

Judge Berman had been appointed to his seat on the District Court for the Southern District of New York by Epstein's former pal, President Bill Clinton. As a steward of the law, Berman wanted to see all of the evidence. He also wanted to hear from Epstein's victims.

But first, and most of all, was the pending question of whether to keep Epstein behind bars.

Court adjourned until his decision could be rendered.

While Judge Berman was considering the evidence, however, a new chapter to the story began. On July 17, an eighteen-year-old woman—identified in her claim as Kaitlyn Doe—filed a lawsuit claiming that Epstein had sexually violated her in October 2008, *while* he was on work release from prison at his West Palm Beach "Florida Science Foundation" office. She claimed that a deputy was standing outside the door the entire time and did nothing to thwart the attack.

According to Doe, the meetings were scheduled to discuss her "necessary surgeries." Not only did Epstein force her to perform sex acts, according to the filing; but also, Doe claimed he demanded that she marry one of his female recruiters—a non-US citizen who needed a green card.

"Jeffrey Epstein, through his brazen and powerful organization, was quite literally able to commit federal sex trafficking offenses at his work release office, during his jail sentence," court documents obtained for this book state.

The victim's attorney, Brad Edwards, came forward to claim that Epstein used his "work" during prison to sucker many women into sex.

"They believed they were going there for something other than a sexual purpose," Edwards said. "Not one of the individuals was a prostitute. These were all people who at that time wanted something. They came over under false pretenses and he manipulated them."

Upon learning about the claim, Florida Governor Ron Desantis ordered an immediate—if woefully belated—investigation into Epstein's work-release program and the Palm Beach County Sheriff's office.

The following day, unsurprisingly, Epstein's request for bail was denied. In his written order, Judge Berman stated:

> The Government's evidence against Mr. Epstein appears strong. The evidence includes testimony of victims, some of whom were minor girls when they were allegedly sexually abused by Mr. Epstein; other witnesses, including potential co-conspirators; physical evidence, including passports reflecting extensive foreign travel; sexually suggestive photographs of nude underage girls; plea discussions; and police reports describing witness tampering and intimidation . . .

This newly discovered evidence also suggests that Mr. Epstein poses ongoing and forward-looking danger. . . . . Mr. Epstein's dangerousness is considerable and includes sex crimes with minor girls and tampering with potential witnesses . . .

Mr. Epstein's alleged excessive attraction to sexual conduct with or in the presence of minor girls—which is said to include his soliciting and receiving massages from young girls and young women perhaps as many as four times a day—appears likely to be uncontrollable . . .

The Court finds that the Government has shown by a preponderance of the evidence that Mr. Epstein is a flight risk. . . . The Court is also concerned for new victims. . . . The Government's motion for remand (detention) is granted and the Defense motion for pretrial release is denied.

Epstein's legal team immediately protested, filing an appeal. Either missing or willfully ignoring the enormous scope of the ruling, they focused on Epstein's fake passport. They claimed it had been used to disguise his Jewish heritage in the Middle East, where he could have been a desirable target for kidnappers. For many, that seemed like a stretch.

A trial date was set for mid-2020 and Epstein was sent back to his cell. The judge ordered that he would stay there up until the trial.

Of course, he would not.

CHAPTER 14

DEAD OR GONE

Nights at the MCC prison were never quite silent. But on July 23, whatever peace that reigned there was shattered at 1:28 am, when guards heard a cry for help coming from within cell #123. They rushed to the cell, peered through the narrow cell door window, and saw inmate 76318–054—Jeffrey Epstein—crumpled in a fetal position on the concrete floor.

His face, feet and hands were light blue. He seemed motionless. He looked dead.

Epstein's cellmate, Nicholas Tartaglione, was still shouting for assistance as the guards opened the door. They entered the cell and ordered the hulking and agitated Tartaglione to turn around. After securing him, the guards grabbed Epstein's limp body and lifted it as if they were about to dispose of an old rug.

Our investigation uncovered a fellow inmate who actually witnessed the incident from across the prison hall.

"The main guy watching Epstein the night he tried to kill himself had always seemed like he didn't want anything to do with him," the cellblock neighbor told us exclusively.

I heard Epstein's bunkie call for help, and when they opened the door I saw Epstein on the floor.

When they carried him out of the cell, they dropped him on the floor face-first. He didn't make a sound because he was out cold. I heard his head hit the floor with a thud. I thought he was dead.

Then they lifted him up cuffed him and dropped him AGAIN—this time face-first on the stretcher. They throw him facedown onto it. It looked like there were marks on his neck. They must have revived him with CPR.

Indeed, the MCC medical staff successfully revived Epstein and kept him in the infirmary for the rest of the evening. They suspected his injuries were due to foul play, but Tartaglione firmly denied that conclusion. He pointed out that he actually saved Epstein's life—a claim our prison witness corroborates.

"I don't think Epstein's cellmate had anything to do with it," the jailmate insisted. "They were good with each other. Epstein's cellmate seemed to watch out for him. There was no way he attacked him."

That left only two other scenarios: Epstein's wounds were self-inflicted. Or, someone else had managed to enter and exit the cell.

Certainly, Epstein's transition from the high life to prison life had been the rockiest of roads. Had he reached his breaking point in the five days since being denied bail? It seems incredibly unlikely. If shape-shifting Epstein had one enduring quality, it was a belief that he was above the law.

That presented the second possibility. One that was much more nefarious. While Epstein tried to silence his victims, was someone else trying to silence *him*?

Certainly, the walls of the MCC would prove no match for a team as sophisticated as the Kremlin or Mossad. At that time, however, it was a line of investigation that the Bureau of Prisons and the Department of Justice—led by William Barr, remember, the son of Epstein's old Dalton connection—did not seem interested in pursuing.

The event had left Epstein startlingly pale and gaunt, but prison officials felt that the neck abrasions didn't reflect an earnest suicide attempt. In their opinion, Epstein had staged the incident to garner sympathy from the court.

Indeed, the marks on his neck were not immediately visible when he appeared in court again just a few days later.

"We don't know at this point whether his injuries are caused by a suicide attempt or an attack by others," victims' attorney Gloria Allred said at the time.

"However he sustained his injuries, we want him to be forced to face a jury and respond to the serious charges that he is facing."

To that end, the MCC's most notorious new inmate was relocated to the more secure suicide prevention wing. But for Epstein, it only made life behind bars worse.

Epstein's new home was a solitary confinement unit, where conditions were even more dire than in 9-South. The few "luxuries" that he had been allowed there were revoked while he sat alone in his suicide-risk room.

All objects that Epstein could potentially use to inflict bodily harm were not allowed. He had no clothing or bed linens to strangle himself with, only a gown and bedding "blanket" made of paper that prevented him from self-harm. He had no books, no mail, and wasn't provided with anything to pass the time. He had a fixed desk and stool, but no reason to use it. He had a shower, but the faucet had an "off" timer to prevent him from drowning himself in a clogged drain. This was by design.

For meals, Epstein was given crude, single-ingredient sandwiches. At night, the lights never went out, so the guard stationed outside his cell could observe him at all times.

Epstein also wasn't allowed visitors or phone calls during his observational period. If he wanted to die, he'd have to—literally—bash his own brains out.

While on suicide watch, Epstein had daily psychiatric evaluations. However, they were very brief in length. A single psychologist serviced both the MCC and the 1,600-inmate Metropolitan Detention Center in Brooklyn, a workload that was obscene by any standard.

After a few days in this veritable torture chamber, the cold reality of his predicament must have set in.

For nearly five decades, Epstein had spoiled himself with an unbroken chain of instant gratification. He did what he wanted, when he wanted, and how he wanted. He ate well and considered restaurants filthy. He practiced yoga and showered several times a day. He slept with the A/C at polar temperatures and started every day with the same special bran muffin. He had butlers, chauffeurs, and private chefs.

Life in the suicide ward, for a soulless individual like Epstein, would have been intolerable. So, as he had done for years, he decided to use someone else to better his situation: He blamed his injuries on cellmate Tartaglione.

"It's simply, patently false to say that Epstein did anything other than try to kill himself," said Tartaglione's attorney Bruce Barket, who confirmed that Epstein and Taraglione were "friends" and that MCC "cleared" his client of wrongdoing.

But Epstein's lawyers convinced prison staff, and he used his silver tongue to convince his shrink that he had been cured—of his suicidal impulses, at least.

"Once an inmate is placed on suicide watch, the watch may only be terminated by a Bureau [of Prisons] psychologist following a face-to-face evaluation of the inmate," Assistant Attorney General Stephen E. Boyd would later confirm.

"Mr. Epstein was later removed from suicide watch after being evaluated by a doctoral-level psychologist who determined that suicide watch was no longer warranted."

But according to forensic psychiatrist Dr. Ziv Cohen, who has made the rounds at MCC, "Any case where someone had a proven or suspected serious suicide attempt, that would be unusual to within two to three weeks take them off suicide watch."

Such protocol is in place to protect the prison's residents. But to some, Epstein's well-being was the last thing on the guards' minds.

"The guards were happy Epstein was trying to kill himself," his jailmate told these authors. "They laughed at him. The guards definitely didn't like

Epstein. I think they took him off suicide watch and put him back on 9-South intentionally."

In any case, on July 29, Epstein shuffled back to his former digs, where he rejoined Tartaglione.

Former warden Cameron Lindsay, who was a member of the US Department of Justice's Senior Executive Service when he retired from the Federal Bureau of Prisons, told reporter Doug Montero that Epstein's speedy removal from suicide watch was "shocking."

"For someone this high profile, with these allegations and this many victims, who has had a suicide attempt in the last few weeks, you can take absolutely no chances," Lindsay explained. "You leave him on suicide watch until he's out of there."

For Epstein, that would be a while. During a brief hearing on July 31, the FBI confirmed that they were actively analyzing the evidence taken from Epstein's Manhattan residence and needed time to thoroughly explore all the material. Judge Berman set Epstein's trial date for June 2020.

Physically, Epstein showed up for the hearing that day; but mentally, the criminal mastermind seemed to be elsewhere. The defendant's notorious smirking lips were stuck in neutral position. He wore thin-framed glasses and a dark blue prison uniform. His elbows rested on the courtroom table and his hands remained locked as if involuntarily begging. He said nothing, he did nothing, and he showed no reaction to the proceedings. For those present, it was a jarring transformation from the super-villain they'd seen before.

"When I saw him come in, he looked out of it," victims' attorney Gloria Allred told reporter Jen Heger about that day in court. "He looked tired, a little bit confused. That's not a surprise given conditions of jail, which are very different than the home of a billionaire."

As FBI agents described the blackmail treasure trove they'd found in Epstein's New York home and on Little St. James, perhaps Epstein was conducting a mental tour of his other properties and hideouts, inventorying what investigators would find at each location—or rather, what he hoped they wouldn't find.

With lots of powerful friends, and even more powerful enemies, Epstein had to wonder if someone would find it all and turn it in to guarantee their freedom. If the situation were reversed, he had to know he would.

Less than thirty minutes after he arrived in the courtroom, Epstein was taken back through the passenger tunnel and locked in his cage.

Summoning a desperate resolve, however, the evil sex villain decided that he still had one more fight in him.

On August 1, Epstein was granted a meeting with his longtime friend David Schoen, an Atlanta-based attorney.

"Mr. Epstein had asked me to take over his defense and I agreed," Schoen told reporter Andy Tillett, "but subject to meeting with his longtime lawyers to see if they would accept me in that role, or if I would have to put together my own team."

When Epstein and Schoen finished their lengthy meeting, they agreed to meet again the following week.

Schoen told Tillett: "We never had that meeting."

Schoen says Epstein was in good spirits, but several witnesses contend that over the next few days, Epstein lost his grip. They described him as "disheveled" and reported that he was "sleeping on the floor . . . like a pig in a sty."

Had he lost it, or was that all another act? Or was he worried about something else entirely?

Whether he knew it or not, Epstein had only forty-eight hours to live.

On August 8, he met with his attorneys to update his last will and testament. Epstein's legal declaration protected his fortune in a sealed trust that could only be distributed to a named Trustee (or Trustees). That meant that only authorized people were allowed to touch what was left of his estate— still a healthy $500 million or more. Unless his victims were named as Trustees, they wouldn't be able to recover any court settlements. It was the perfect plan.

The executors would be his longtime lawyers, Darren K. Indyke and Richard D. Kahn. Each would receive $250,000 for their efforts. Oddly, Epstein named biotech entrepreneur and Harvard immunologist Boris Nikolic as a backup. Nikolic claims he has no idea why Epstein would have named him in the document.

However, the men once moved in similar circles. Nikolic was chief scientific adviser to Epstein friend Bill Gates, who had close ties to Epstein for many years.

Gates has insisted, "I didn't have any business relationship or close personal friendship with him," but a recently uncovered photograph shows Gates with Nikolic inside Epstein's NYC mansion, alongside former Treasury Secretary and President of Harvard, Larry Summers. *The New York Times* found that that visit was one of several during 2011, with at least one continuing "late into the night." The paper reported that Gates emailed colleagues at the time: "His lifestyle is very different and kind of intriguing although it would not work for me." (A rep claimed his email referred to Epstein's interior design.)

After his first visit to Epstein's home, on January 31, 2011, Gates reportedly emailed colleagues: "A very attractive Swedish woman and her daughter dropped by and I ended up staying there quite late."

That woman was reportedly former Ms. Sweden Eva Andersson-Dubin, and her fifteen-year-old daughter. Epstein appeared to have had an affinity for the girl. At least two times in documents obtained from his home, the handwritten phrase "Eva's little girl on the boat," appears, totally without any other context.

The next month, Gates and Epstein were spotted chatting in Long Beach at the TED conference. They were back in New York by May, when Gates again visited Epstein's home and bragged about it over email.

Also at the May meeting was James Staley, a high-ranking JP Morgan official. JP Morgan and Gates's foundation were then in talks to create the Global Health Investment Fund, which would support the development of health-related technologies around the world. Epstein was desperate to get involved, reportedly insisting to potential partners that his status as a registered sex offender should not affect the potential deal: According to the *New York Times*, he said at one gathering that his crimes had been "no worse than stealing a bagel."

That deal never materialized, but Epstein and Gates saw each other several times in New York and Palm Beach as late as 2014. They did not see each other in the years leading up to Epstein's most recent arrest.

Did Gates's adviser stay in touch? He insists he was "shocked" to find himself named as a backup executor for Epstein's estate. No matter the logic behind that choice, Epstein's decision to put his assets in a trust would lock the money in a special account. Its origins would be untraceable, and his agents could utilize the funds for his defense, comfort, or even bribes. Epstein was taking positive action, putting players and pieces in motion.

The very next day, on August 9, Epstein was blindsided by a new threat: a court had voted 2-to-1 to unseal all files relating to Virginia Roberts Giuffre's 2017 defamation lawsuit against Ghislaine. The voluminous document dump was fast and furious, exposing the shocking extent of Epstein's perversions and his network of rich, famous, and powerful sexual predator pals. Everyone from Prince Andrew to the Palm Beach police were about to get taken down.

Reporters scrambled to comb through the documents, finding new allegations and new names, such as former New Mexico governor Bill Richardson, billionaire Glenn Dubin, and former Democratic Senate Majority Leader George Mitchell. Roberts claimed Epstein forced her to have sex with all those men—a claim they all denied. The unsealing seemed like a shot across the bow to Epstein and his coconspirators. It was about to get ugly. Most of all, for Epstein.

In his cell that evening, as Epstein pondered what horrors were to come, his cellmate was not there. For some reason, Tartaglione had been moved to another unit, and Epstein had not been assigned another. Both of those developments were highly unusual, and the reason for those decisions is unclear. No matter why, Epstein was alone—and no one was watching.

During the overnight shift, MCC had eighteen guards holding down the entire facility. Built for just 474 souls, the facility was known in recent years to be stuffed with up to eight hundred. As a result, many of the workers had to put in overtime. That night, the 9-South guards tasked with watching Epstein were on that list. One had logged eighty hours that week working "doubles." The other was a former correctional officer who volunteered to pick up shifts at the understaffed institution.

Although both men were low-level staff members, they had to have known that Epstein was the most vital to prosecutors. In addition, they could not have been ignorant of the fact that Epstein had almost died just days ago. Unfortunately, both coincidentally decided that something else was more important.

For three hours beginning at 3:30 a.m., the 9-South guards failed to do six mandatory visual checks on Epstein. These rounds were to occur every thirty minutes. Not one happened. According to Bureau of Prisons officials, the two guards happened to fall asleep at their posts, at the exact same time and for the exact same duration.

At approximately 6:20 a.m., the guards awoke and began their breakfast rounds. When they looked in on Epstein at 6:25, they saw the full weight of his body suspended by a bedsheet that was twisted around his doughy throat.

The guards hurriedly entered the cell. One of them severed the knotted sheet that connected the inmate to the top bunk while the other guard triggered an alarm.

They let Epstein drop like an anchor.

The sex felon's cold, rigid body had turned a chilling blue and he was unmistakably lifeless. He had been dead for a while.

Radios throughout the prison blasted, "Body alarm on South. Body alarm on South."

At 6:33 a.m., EMS took control of the situation and administered CPR. They knew immediately, however, that there was no bringing him back.

Nevertheless, Jeffrey Edward Epstein was taken to New York Presbyterian Lower Manhattan Hospital, where he was pronounced dead at 7:36 a.m.

Even though Epstein was found hanged, his cause of death was listed as: *"Pending Further Study."*

As his body was being wheeled to the medical examiner, a *New York Post* street photographer managed to snap one last scandalous photo of the monster.

But even that would not be enough to convince the world that Epstein was dead.

A verdict of suicide was not sufficient to answer the many lingering questions.

Why was Epstein on suicide watch one week—and remarkably, off of it the next?

Why, on the night of Epstein's death, was his cellmate gone?

Why would a suicidal man *ever* have been left alone?

Why was the camera outside Epstein's cell "broken"?

Why did the guards fall asleep at exactly the same time, and then later falsify their logs?

When the autopsy report was finalized, there were even *more* questions.

New York City Chief Medical Examiner Dr. Barbara Sampson completed her examination in roughly twenty-four hours, but then announced she was not ready to release her findings.

"The ME's (Medical Examiner's) determination is pending further information at this time," she said in a public statement. "My office defers to the involved law enforcement agencies regarding other investigations around this death."

The examiner also added this unusual tidbit: *"At the request of those representing the decedent (Epstein), and with the awareness of the federal prosecutor, I allowed a private pathologist (Dr. Michael Baden) to observe the autopsy examination."*

Epstein's lawyers had asked Dr. Baden to confirm their client's cause of death. The infamous former New York chief medical examiner had also been an expert witness for O. J. Simpson during the football legend's high-stakes murder trial in 1995, and was chairman of the House Select Committee on Assassinations' Forensic Pathology Panel that investigated the assassination of John F. Kennedy.

The question on many minds was this: Why would Dr. Sampson need an observer?

Did the dead man's representatives fear she would tamper with the findings for some unarticulated reason?

Or did the estate hope to have a hand in shaping those findings for some purpose of their own?

After carefully reviewing "all investigative information, including complete autopsy findings," Dr. Sampson declared on August 16 that Jeffrey Epstein had, in fact, hanged himself.

"In all forensic investigations, all information must be synthesized to determine the cause and manner of death," she stated. "Everything must be consistent; no single finding can be evaluated in a vacuum."

The official story was that Epstein had secured one end of his bedsheet around his neck. It would have been sturdy enough to do so, since he had been moved off suicide watch, with its paper sheets. Then, the ME claimed, he tied the other end to the top bunk in cell #123, and leaned forward.

In the process, sources told the *Washington Post*, Epstein broke several bones in his neck, including his hyoid, a small U-shaped bone above the Adam's apple that helps keep your throat open.

That particular detail was explosive. Although a broken hyoid does occur in 27 percent of suicides by hanging, it's more often seen in cases where there is great force applied during the event, such as someone jumping from a height. That is, a hanging unlike Epstein's supposed lean into death.

Hyoid breaks are much more common in other incidents; they occur in 50 percent of all murders by strangulation.

Questions swirled even faster with that revelation. Adding tension to the doubt and fear in the air, Epstein's own family was not given a copy of the autopsy report, leaving them unable to confirm or rule out the *Post's* bombshell reporting.

"We are not satisfied with the conclusions of the medical examiner," Epstein's attorneys said in a statement. "We will have a more complete response in the coming days."

Even with so much at stake, the world and even Epstein's family was forced to wait. Nearly two weeks after the medical examiner released the findings of the report, we learned from a source close to Epstein's legal team that his family had not been given a copy of the official report.

"Family lawyers were calling the NYC Medical Examiner daily," the insider told investigator Jen Heger. "It is extremely unusual to have issued a death certificate, but not to have given a copy of the autopsy report to the family."

"The family is entitled to a copy per New York law before it's made public," the source added. "Clearly that did not happen in this case."

"The Medical Examiner just kept putting off the lawyers, saying, 'It's not ready yet,' but the death certificate couldn't have been issued without a completed autopsy report. It was clear they were stalling."

In the meantime, in response to growing public demand, United States Attorney General William Barr took action. Barr—the son of Epstein's old Dalton pal—reassigned MCC Warden Lamine N'Diaye and the acting head of the US Bureau of Prisons, Hugh Hurwitz.

The MCC put the two negligent 9-South guards—whose names have been kept confidential—on administrative leave. Criminal investigators subpoenaed over a dozen MCC employees, as the Department of Justice vowed to uncover the truth.

"We will get to the bottom of what happened, and there will be accountability," an angry and embarrassed Barr told the public. "Let me assure you that this case will continue on against anyone who was complicit with Epstein."

In the months to come, however, the news of the DOJ investigation was minimal. The public was left to decide on their own what really happened inside the Metropolitan Corrections Center that fateful night.

In the course of this investigation, we spoke to dozens of people. When asked, every person close to the case believed at the time of this writing that his death was *NOT* a suicide.

EPSTEIN VICTIMS' ATTORNEY GLORIA ALLRED: "At this point, I don't feel there are enough facts to say definitively that it was suicide. Even though the medical examiner for the city of New York, who did the autopsy, has ruled that the cause of death was suicide, I'm not prepared to say without knowing all the facts and that we can 100 percent conclude that it is suicide.

"Again, there are more questions than answers, and I'm not going to engage in a conspiracy theory, but I would like to know what all the facts are. Now in court, I did agree with the defense that their needs to be more of an investigation.

"Even if we thought it was an attempted suicide attempt [the first time], that should have been a red flag to protect him. So, there are more questions than answers at this point.

"Why the three fractures in his neck consistent with suicide, but also consistent with strangulation?

"Why were the guards not checking every thirty minutes?

"Why did he not have a cellmate at that time?

"Were the guards' records where they were supposedly monitoring him tampered with and changed?

"Why would the guards, some of them, claim the Fifth and not provide interviews to the investigators?

"This is a major, major problem.

EPSTEIN VICTIMS' ATTORNEY LISA BLOOM: "I'm not ready to conclude that it was suicide. The fact that he had just changed his will, I think a couple days before, is significant to me that does point toward suicide. But . . . I'm going to take it at face value, say, "He sure wasn't acting like somebody who was going to kill himself!" . . .

"The injuries to his neck could have been from suicide. It also could have been from somebody strangling him. I know from the many, many murder cases that I used to cover on Court TV where I for eight years watched murder cases, a medical examiner saying it's suicide, it's really an opinion. And there are probably also medical examiners who would say, "Well it's not suicide.""

"So I think there should be at least a second or a third opinion by an objective medical examiner. I think we should get to the bottom of it and there should be a full investigation.

EPSTEIN VICTIMS' ATTORNEY SPENCER KUVIN: "When Mr. Epstein was reported to be deceased, my clients, obviously had some hesitation as to whether or not it was accurate or whether or not this was another disappearing act by Mr. Epstein, some elaborate scheme to be able to get out of all of this. . . .

"Personally, knowing what I know about the system and about the jail that he was in, there are a number of things that I question. Professionally and speaking with people that have worked inside jails like this, I question, number one, how is it possible that they don't have video of what occurred? I was contacted even after his supposed death by a guard that worked inside of the MCC that was adamant that every section and square inch of that jail is covered by cameras.

"We now know through reporting that at least two cameras were sent to the FBI crime lab because they were supposedly broken or not working correctly. You couldn't write it better in a crime novel, it just doesn't make sense. A lot of it doesn't make sense.

"It doesn't make sense how he was taken off a suicide watch. It doesn't make sense that his one cellmate that he had, that could have possibly prevented anything like this or been witness to something like this, was moved out just a day before the incident occurs.

"It doesn't make sense that two guards that are supposed to be watching him are supposedly sleeping and just gone for hours. None of it makes sense.

"I question, number one, most importantly, is it true? Did he somehow pull off a Houdini and somehow just disappear despite all of the reporting and despite all of the evidence that came out and despite all the information that's out there?

"Second, I question . . . who got paid? Because someone clearly, likely got paid off. Someone, somewhere has got some secret account offshore that has a lot of money in it now, that didn't before he was dead. . . . whether someone actually took him out so that he couldn't talk, so that he couldn't tell stories that he knew about people who are powerful, rich, famous, royalty, whatever it may be, we'll never know.

"Unless, of course, there are some videos somewhere, again, that exist, that are in the hands of the federal government or the FBI of what happened inside that jail on that morning.

EPSTEIN FRIEND, ATTORNEY DAVID SCHOEN: "I also don't believe it was suicide. I don't believe conspiracy theories either, but I don't believe suicide for several reasons."

Interview after interview, we heard the most respected minds in the country attest that Epstein's death could not have been a suicide. Except, that is, for one: Epstein's former attorney and friend Alan Dershowitz.

We asked Dershowitz point-blank: "Do you believe these conspiracy theories that somebody else came in and killed him?"

Dershowitz was unequivocal in his response:

I'm not a conspiracy person. . . . The simplest, most obvious explanation is that he decided he didn't want to spend the rest of his life in prison. He didn't think he was going to have a fair shot, and decided to take his own life.

I think it would've been virtually impossible for anybody to get into the prison. If he had been with a cellmate, that might be different. But alone in the prison, locked door, even with sleeping guards, I think the most likely explanation is the most obvious one, that he tried to kill himself and then ultimately succeeded.

Even Dershowitz, however, had one caveat: "I think you should always second-guess any governmental investigation. I don't think they're going to find anything very different about the cause of death. I think that an investigation might, however, find some things about the circumstances that would allow him to take his own life."

***

When it comes to the circumstances of Epstein's death, the incident bears a striking similarity to the notorious death of one of the twenty-first century's most famous Mossad agents.

Ben Zygier was born in Australia in 1976, and reportedly became an agent of the Mossad in the early 2000s, when he was working as a businessman in the Middle East. In early 2010, it was reported that he had been imprisoned in Israel for threatening to expose other Mossad agents. The conditions of his confinement were so secretive that he was known simply as "Mr. X" to guards.

By the end of that year, Mr. X was dead, via "suicide." Like Epstein, Zygier had met with his attorneys shortly before his death, and was said to be in good spirits at the time. Despite a history of suicide attempts, he had been placed in a cell that was not suicide-proof, and had no cellmate. Supposedly, he used his sheet to tie a noose to the bars of his window, and killed himself by leaning forward. Members of the rescue crew claimed he had been able to do it out of view of the security cameras that swept his cell.

Amid public outcry following his death, an Israeli judge conducted an investigation and found "orders had been given to prevent suicide" and "these were not upheld." The judge also found strange bruises on Zygier's body and traces of a tranquilizer drug in his system. She ultimately concluded that she "could not rule out the intervention of another person who intentionally caused his death."

At the end of it all, the Israeli government reportedly paid his family $1 million.

Despite rumors that Epstein's death may have been a hit by the Mossad, the method of his death does not seem to carry the fingerprints of Israel's secret security force, which tends to prefer simple shootings. In the list of confirmed Israeli assassinations since 1970, there is not one incident of strangulation. (The Israeli government has a policy stating that targeted killings are legal.)

What about other killer spies? The Kremlin obviously seems to prefer poisoning. The MI6 claims they do not carry out assassinations at all—a lie. The only nation with a history of mysterious deaths by strangulation is one heavily linked to Epstein: Saudi Arabia.

At the time of this writing, the murder of *Washington Post* journalist Jamal Khashoggi—strangled by a Saudi hit squad in an Istanbul embassy— still dominates the headlines. But it isn't the first scandalous Saudi strangling.

We have uncovered that way back in 1986, a Saudi Royal Family relative was found strangled to death in a hotel room across the Potomac River from Washington, D.C. An *AP* report at the time said police "had established no suspects or motives in the slaying."

In February 2010, Saudi Prince Saud Abdulaziz bin Nasser al Saud was convicted of murder and sentenced to life in prison after strangling his aide to death in a hotel room. In 2013, he was flown back to Saudi Arabia, where it was said that he would serve out the rest of his sentence.

In 2011, well-known Shia spiritual leader Usama Al-Atar claimed he had been strangled nearly to death in prison after his arrest while making a hajj pilgrimage to Medina. Insisting his arrest had been motivated by religious extremism, the Canadian citizen was later freed when his government intervened.

Epstein's links to Saudi Arabia during his time as an arms trader in the 1980s and early 1990s—led by Iran Contra kingpin Adnan Khashoggi—are beyond dispute. But new reporting has placed him in Riyadh even more recently.

Flight data obtained by this investigative team shows that just hours before the United States 2016 election that would elect President Donald J. Trump, Epstein's jet flew from Paris to Riyadh, where it landed at 6:35 p.m. local time.

Two days later, at 3:47 p.m. local time on November 9, the same aircraft departed the Saudi capital, flying in the opposite direction back to Paris. At the time, it would have been 8:47 a.m. in New York—not long before Hillary Clinton would concede to Trump.

Epstein's friend and colleague, Prince Mohammed Bin Salman, was in Riyadh at the time. (Epstein kept a personal photo of him in his Manhattan home.)

Also in Riyadh over that period was Amazon founder Jeff Bezos, who met with MBS and advisers on November 9.

Epstein and Bezos were already acquaintances, having both attended the Edge foundation "billionaire's dinner" in 2011 and 2014, years after Epstein pleaded guilty to soliciting underage prostitution.

It's unclear if Epstein met with any of the men, or what he might have said. What aspect of the Trump/Clinton election would have necessitated an unusual quickie trip to Riyadh?

What's more, what aspect of Trump's unthinkable win made it possible for Epstein to return to Paris?

If Clinton had been elected, would he have stayed in Saudi Arabia? He did have a fake passport listing his residence as in the Middle Eastern country.

Was Epstein afraid of the Clintons in the years before his arrest and death?

Or someone else?

CHAPTER 15

ONCE UPON A TIME IN RUSSIA

In the hours and days following the announcement of Jeffrey Epstein's death, people across America were watching closely for reports about what exactly had happened. So, it seems, was the Kremlin, also known as the lair of President Vladimir Putin.

As the news broke, many social media accounts confirmed to be Russian bots began actively promoting salacious and bizarre conspiracy theories surrounding Epstein's death. The Russian state television channel, RT, led off one nightly broadcast with some of the more outrageous claims. Even President Trump got in on the action, retweeting a post from conservative commentator Terrence K. Williams that read:

> Died of SUICIDE on 24/7 SUICIDE WATCH? Yeah right! How does that happen#JefferyEpstein had information on Bill Clinton & now he's dead
> I see #TrumpBodyCount trending but we know who did this! RT if you're not Surprised#EpsteinSuicide #ClintonBodyCount #ClintonCrimeFamily

Senator Marco Rubio, a member of the Senate Intelligence Committee, confirmed that Russian bots and trolls were actively promoting such outlandish theories.

"The immediate rush to spread conspiracy theories about someone on the 'other side' of partisan divide having him killed illustrates why our society is so vulnerable to foreign disinformation and influence efforts," Rubio tweeted.

"It's sad (and frightening) to see so many Americans on both sides . . . unwittingly helping them," he continued, adding that Putin "has weaponized our polarization."

But why would Putin have a stake in promoting conspiracy theories about Epstein's death?

In one interpretation, it could have been a simple smoke screen, meant to obscure the truth. In another, it could have been a deterrent aimed at anyone asking further questions about the nature of his death.

Who would publicly question the official suicide story when it would mean being lumped in with a bunch of Kremlin bots? Having the courage to do so might require some additional assurance, some inside proof.

***

John Mark Dougan, a former Palm Beach County Deputy Sheriff, told our team that he's certain Epstein was murdered—and he knows why.

"I don't believe for one minute it was suicide," he said.

The world's intelligence agencies couldn't risk the chance of Epstein's blackmail files ever going public, Dougan claims. Those files are explosive, and he knows. Because he has them.

Dougan served as a Deputy Sheriff in Palm Beach at the time Epstein was in prison after securing his secret plea deal. Now, he lives in Russia, where he has been granted political asylum.

Epstein's prison time "was an absolute shitshow," Dougan told author James Robertson from the dark streets of Moscow. "I'll tell you why. He was able to leave jail basically anytime he wanted. Right? This is really unheard of.

"But he was able to leave jail as long as he had two deputies go with him on an overtime detail. They were paid as an overtime detail. Now, overtime detail, this is Palm Beach County Sheriff's Office, by contract are selected out of a random pool. This was different. These deputies that would go with him were handpicked by the sheriff. And there were guys specifically who would look the other way while he was bringing underage girls into his office and into his home. Unbelievable."

Palm Beach Police Detective Joseph Recarey had run the initial investigation into Epstein's crimes. But once in prison, the case was under the jurisdiction of the Sheriffs. Dougan says Recarey gave him full access to everything he knew about the infamous inmate.

"We basically had the entire case file," he said. According to Dougan, Recarey also gave him materials that were not in the "official" filings as well.

When asked if he was aware of any blackmail tapes made by Epstein, Dougan was unequivocal:

> Absolutely. They weren't tapes so much as DVDs. I don't know if these were footages or not, but every bedroom in Epstein's houses had multiple cameras in them.
>
> He used to keep records of everybody. He used to store everything. So the Palm Beach Police Department, they knew that there were thousands and thousands of these DVDs. Except . . . Now, this is very interesting.
>
> When they went to search for them, they were gone.
>
> It's not really a question of who would have had access. The question you should be asking is: Who had knowledge that the search was coming? And the answer to that is the Palm Beach County State Attorney's Office and the Palm Beach County Sheriff's Office. Because the State Attorney's Office and Sheriff's Office, they're the ones who have to take the warrants and take them in front of the judge to get them signed off. There were elements within these two organizations that didn't want to see anything happen to Epstein.

How far would Epstein's protectors go to keep their prized asset safe?

Joseph Recarey, the police officer who had original access to the black-mail files, died suddenly after a "brief illness" at the age of fifty in 2018.

"It's funny, because back in May when everything started to happen with Epstein again, when all the ruckus started to get raised again, he mysteriously died," Dougan said. "I knew this guy, man. He was fit as a fiddle. He was fifty years old. And he died of a sudden illness. That's what they wrote. 'He died of a sudden illness.' It was unexplained."

Two years before, Dougan had fled for Russia, taking his own tranche of the tapes with him. He still has them today. Encrypted. Hidden.

"Do I think that Epstein was probably put up to getting some wealthy people to sleep with some underage women so those people could be black-mailed by Western intelligence agencies? Absolutely I do," he said.

Among those targets, Dougan claims, was Prince Andrew. A September 2019 report in Britain's *Times of London* revealed that the MI6 were "concerned that Russia may have obtained kompromat, compromising material, on Prince Andrew."

Dougan insisted to our team that he is not a Russian asset. But in any case, the Kremlin is likely very happy to have the Epstein blackmail files within their borders.

After the claims about Prince Andrew surfaced, Dougan released the following statement:

> Although we worked in different law enforcement agencies, former Town of Palm Beach Police Department Detective Joe Recarey, who was the lead detective on the solicitation-of-minors case against billionaire Jeffrey Epstein, was a friend. I was shocked, as were family and friends, to learn of his unexpected death at age 50 just over a year ago.
>
> Joe Recarey was very aware of my efforts to uncover breaches of public trust by the Palm Beach County Sheriff's office via my award-winning investigative website. In late 2009 or early 2010, Joe asked me to scan all the documents as well as copy hundreds

of DVD disks he had on the Jeffrey Epstein case to keep them safe. He had lost faith in Barry Krischer, the Palm Beach County state's attorney at the time of the investigation. I would meet with him occasionally to get more documents to store, the last time being in 2015.

I have never looked at what was given to me by Joe Recarey, other than the file names, types, and sizes. The FBI seized my computers in 2016 which had everything Recarey gave me. The FBI and other intelligence agencies may be surprised to have discovered that I kept an off-site backup that was sent to me in 2017, after I was safely established in Russia.

According to news reports, US intelligence agencies apparently analyzed the files and communicated with British authorities. If Britain's Secret Intelligence Service, commonly known as MI6, has concerns about any ties between Prince Andrew and Jeffrey Epstein, they got it from their Washington counterparts, not me.

Of course, this means the FBI has seen everything and has more knowledge of the contents than I do because it was not my business to look deep into the files: I was simply acting as Joe Recarey's computer "safety deposit box." It also means that the FBI has the same exact data that I possess and are in a position to know everyone who is implicated in the videos, recordings, and documents. If media reports are accurate, it seems the FBI has knowledge that Epstein files involve Prince Andrew in some manner, since they made it a point to contact MI6 and warn them.

The Epstein data is encrypted in a TrueCrypt/VeraCrypt container and has been given to a few people. They cannot look at the contents because they do not have the decryption keys. Others have the decryption keys, but they do not have access to the encrypted containers. My contacts are on five continents and do not know each other. The Epstein files stay secure and unreadable to everyone. I do not have a physical copy in my immediate possession, because of security reasons.

This is to make sure my family and friends remain safe. I have made arrangements that it can only be decrypted in the event of my arrest, if I go missing for an extended time, or in case of my unusual or untimely demise. I have a system in place to connect people with the encrypted containers to those who have the decryption keys.

I have made elaborate security precautions because of ongoing legal issues, threats, and harassment. The FBI has tried to arrest me twice since I've been in Moscow by pushing Interpol via a sealed indictment. Both times they failed. Last year, the FBI sent 10 agents and Federal Marshals to a US company that I do contract work for, unsuccessfully trying to intimidate them.

I will not be divulging any of the information I may know of or possess, because the secrecy of the data I have access ensures the safety of me and my loved ones. I hope the growing concerns and reports about Jeffrey Epstein's international sex-trafficking empire, and his relationship with the rich and powerful people like the Duke of York, will generate official and news media investigations which will uncover all the facts.

Not long after releasing that statement, Dougan took matters into his own hands, inviting journalist Ron Chepesiuk to review the materials and confirm their existence. A longtime friend of Dougan, Chepesiuk flew to Moscow on September 24, 2019.

There, according to Chepesiuk, Dougan cracked open the Epstein blackmail files for the very first time.

"He just wanted to verify," Chepesiuk told our team. "He suggested it and I said, 'It's to verify that they have something there.' He said, 'I'm not going to show it to you long.'"

What happened next shocked the journalist:

So what happened was, it was less than five minutes, and a couple of random scenes from the thing. It was obviously surveillance tape of a bedroom and there were a couple of younger, may even have been underage, I don't know, they were very young.

It was far away and it looked like it was coming from a wall. The camera and all that. It looked like surveillance in a TV show. So I just assumed that it was coming from a camera probably facing, on a wall."

And there was some older men and I didn't look at them. It was very hard to see it from afar. I wanted to, but they were definitely dealing with some sex, you know? So that was it. Then he closed it up, and took it again and saved whatever he was doing. I didn't want to know.

I didn't want to have the responsibility of trying to identify people so I wasn't really interested in trying to identify people. I just wanted to look at it and verify that it was what it looked like, surveillance tapes.

Pretty disgusting. Didn't want to be a voyeur. I'm not into that sort of thing. That was it. That was it. It was verified, and that was it.

I guess he wanted to have somebody else say that he had them. We had developed a good working relationship and he trusted me. He just wanted to verify that, because I don't think he ever looked at the tapes until that moment because he got them from this guy in law enforcement in Palm Beach. He never, what I can gather, really was interested in the contents.

He was a straight shooter, he gave his word that he would take care of them, and that's what he did. But he wasn't really interested in what was going on inside.

But he's been forced to pay more attention to it because of what broke in England with the Prince Andrew connection.

That's also the reason, Dougan says, that he fears for his life.

"Now I have the very peculiar problem of worrying about being hunted down by MI6," he claimed.

Chepesiuk said that during his visit, there were indeed red flags.

"John said that he noticed a car following him," he recalled.

"Here in Moscow there's a lot of twists and turns so if you're moving, twisting and turning and here's a car that's always on your, always in sight, you begin to wonder if that car is following you."

"John said the car was behind him right back into the city. It's about thirty or forty kilometers. It's way out there that the alternative airport route in Moscow. So it was a long journey to have this car in the back of you all this way."

Dougan says he's right to be concerned. Recarey's sudden death in 2018—at the age of fifty—shocked those who knew him, as well as those who have followed the Epstein case.

Few people have noted, however, that he was not the only mysterious death in the Palm Beach area during that period. In April 2018, almost exactly one month before Recarey's death, attorney Alan Ross, who represented an Epstein victim in the early civil suits, died of a similarly fast-acting cancer at age sixty-eight.

Before that, the houseman who cleaned Epstein's sex toys, Alfredo Rodriguez, died of a fast-acting, six-month cancer in 2015, almost exactly at the same time as Virginia Roberts Giuffre's civil case brought the Epstein story—and Prince Andrew's part in it—back into the open. He was only sixty.

"Of course, he knew all about Prince Andrew," Rodriguez's widow, Patricia Dunn said at the time.

Recarey's Floridian wife told *Epstein: Dead Men Tell No Tales* that he passed from cancer, too.

Was it just a coincidence that these three men, all in Florida, died similar deaths that seemed timed to developments in the Epstein case? Poisoning by arsenic, heavy metals, and radioactive substances are all known to cause cancer in humans.

Dougan says he's not taking any chances. His family left behind in the United States, he wonders if he'll ever see them again.

"Look, somebody has to expose the evil people, I guess you would say. Somebody's gotta do it, right? And somebody has to pay the price. Am I happy that I've done what I've done? Yeah. I'm very happy with what I've done so far."

"But now you're asking me, is it worth it for me to have lost my children? I don't know, man. I mean, no."

With the blackmail tapes now in the Kremlin's grasp and with the potential to circulate worldwide, some now have a lot more to lose.

CHAPTER 16

THE COCONSPIRATORS

Less than six months before the 2016 election, reporters covering the presidential campaign trail were rocked by an incoming missile: An anonymous woman listed as "Katie Johnson" filed a lawsuit in California accusing Epstein of raping her at his Manhattan home back in 1994, when she was just thirteen.

The claims were similar to those in other lawsuits that had been filed against Epstein in the past, except for one thing: Donald Trump was listed as an alleged coconspirator and fellow rapist.

The moment the lawsuit came across our collective computer screens in the newsroom of employer American Media, Inc., our team sprang into action. Author Howard summoned reporters Melissa Cronin, Doug Montero, Sharon Churcher, Gina Bacchiocchi, and Robert Hartlein to investigate.

Court documents listed Johnson's address in Twentynine Palms, California, not far from author Cronin's Palm Springs home. Speeding out to knock on Johnson's door, Cronin's mind raced with questions: Who would she find there? After covering Epstein's crimes for years, would this be the moment to crack it all open?

Flying through the desert in her car on speakerphone with the reporting team in New York, Cronin turned onto a dusty side street. She had beaten every other reporter there. But she didn't find Johnson. Instead, at the lawsuit's address was a boarded-up, abandoned home. Neighbors called it a "crack house," and said it had most recently been occupied by squatters.

Canvassing businesses in the small, windswept town, Cronin found that no one had ever heard of a "Katie Johnson," nor knew anything about the lawsuit, Epstein, or Trump. Indeed, a "neighbor," Danny Mira, told us that no one had lived at the home since its owner, David Stacey, died in October the year prior.

Mira said he and other neighbors had kept a close watch on the home because it was overrun by drug addicts who squatted there while Stacey was hospitalized in the final days of his life.

The neighbors, with the help of police, managed to clean up the home several months before Stacey's death. Sharon Rose, a local Realtor, told us the property went into default shortly after Stacey's death and was officially taken over by the bank on April 11—fifteen days before the woman filed her suit.

What's more, the phone number the woman listed on the court documents was not connected, and she also told the court she had less than $300 to her name in savings.

It was clear the lawsuit was some kind of a red herring. Speculation ran wild: Had the Clintons planted this to smear Trump and torpedo his campaign? Had Trump planted this in a canny bit of reverse psychology? (I.e. If the suit were dismissed for being fake, other claims against him would seem fake and illegitimate as well.)

The truth was even stranger. The man behind the Katie Johnson lawsuit was a former Jerry Springer producer who called himself "Al Taylor," a.k.a. notorious gossip peddler Norm Lubow. (Lubow was also behind a 2011 story that claimed Justin Bieber had impregnated a fan, Mariah Yeater.)

Lubow's wingman was a conservative antiabortion donor, Steve Baer, who also happened to be a "Never Trumper." Taylor claimed to have met Johnson and heard her story at a party several years before.

Her attorney, Tom Meagher, said she was motivated to come forward at last, with Taylor's backing, to ensure that her rapist would not become president.

Trump's team told author Howard the accusations in the lawsuit were "unequivocally false" and "politically motivated." Even for Trump skeptics, the entire lawsuit seemed fishy from the start.

First, why had she filed from a nonexistent address? Why had no one seemed to have ever met her?

An attorney that represented Johnson admitted even he had trouble tracking her down. For reporters, it was just as difficult.

Journalist Emily Shugerman said Johnson's reps promised her a video interview with the plaintiff, only to cancel on her several times. Were we all being catfished?

Armed with this information, author Howard told attorney Lisa Bloom that our own investigation was turning up red flags, and warned Bloom of a lack of corroborating evidence. These types of conversations are routine in the world of journalism, and *New York Times* reporters have revealed that they also warned Bloom in this case.

Bloom waded in regardless, and announced that she would unveil Johnson at a press conference in November 2016, just days before the election.

When the hour came, Johnson was nowhere to be found.

"Jane Doe has received numerous threats today. . . . She has decided she is too afraid to show her face," Bloom told the gathered reporters. "We're going to have to reschedule."

The case was soon dismissed in California for procedural issues, and "Johnson" refiled in New York, only to drop it again.

Today, many still believe that the Katie Johnson suit was another case of a victim silenced by the crushing jaws of the justice system, another clever escape for Epstein and Trump.

However, our team has been unable to confirm that "Katie Johnson" ever existed. For us, the whole caper is eerily reminiscent of the conspiracy trolls that surfaced after Epstein's death. Plant one crazy fake lawsuit about an Epstein coconspirator, and all the other potential revelations seem just as insane by association.

When approached in an effort to learn the truth about Johnson, Taylor told Howard: "You know I have details about the Clintons' involvement in the whole Katie Johnson affair." He refused to go on further for fear of retribution from those involved in what he characterized as a fictitious scheme.

By the time "Katie" had first appeared in 2016, however, Epstein's real coconspirators must have been getting nervous.

Depositions in the Jane Doe case and Virginia Roberts Giuffre's lawsuit continued to reveal new allegations and names on an almost weekly basis. In 2015, Giuffre's claims against Prince Andrew had dropped a bombshell on Buckingham Palace (claims he, of course, denied).

***

Ever since Epstein's 2008 plea deal secured immunity for his "unnamed co-conspirators," the world had wondered who those people were. With his death in August 2019, it seemed as if the world might never know.

For Epstein victim Michelle Licata, it was chilling:

> He wouldn't have been able to commit suicide. Would he have been able to be murdered? Sure.
>
> I mean, there are a lot of people that are just walking around like, 'You need to shut this down. . . . He is blowing my cover,' is what it felt like.
>
> It was like all these people's dirty secret started coming out one after another after another. I can see those people that are the people that are paying to keep themselves out of jail and out of prison.
>
> Those people are like, "Look I don't care what it takes. You need to shut this up. You need to, I don't know, make him disappear. Make the story disappear. Make these girls be quiet." That's what's happening.
>
> I mean, it seems like they are letting us talk, but that's what's happening.

Will those coconspirators let the victims keep talking forever? This investigation has learned of death threats to at least one victim who spoke out recently.

In addition, victim Alicia Arden told us that she fears she has been black-listed from working in the entertainment world since filing her police report.

"I feel that I may have been blacklisted by Jeffrey Epstein's network. I thought, did someone say something? 'Oh we don't want to work with Alicia, because if we do anything to her, she'll go file a police report.' So I thought that that could have blacklisted me a little," she told author Cronin.

"Because the girls that you see now, that have other Hollywood predators in the news, I don't see them working very much. They've brought up what happened to them, and they've talked about what happened to them, and they've been blacklisted. Why shouldn't we be able to come out and talk about that?"

Meanwhile, the US Attorney's Office for the Southern District of New York, at least, has vowed to continue the fight to bring coconspirators to justice.

On the day of Epstein's death, Manhattan US Attorney Geoffrey Berman released a statement that said: "To those brave young women who have already come forward and to the many others who have yet to do so, let me reiterate that we remain committed to standing for you, and our investigation of the conduct charged in the Indictment—which included a conspiracy count—remains ongoing."

Attorney Gloria Allred revealed to our team:

When I was in court while we were waiting for the court hearing to begin, I spoke with the United States Attorney, Mr. Berman, before the hearing began, and I introduced him to my client in the courtroom, and he did assure them in my presence and he assured me that they are continuing their investigation of any potential co-conspirators.

We should always keep in mind that when Mr. Epstein was indicted in this latest proceeding, there also in the indictment was not only the indictment of Mr. Epstein but the indictment also talked about unnamed co-conspirators. So even before his death, the Justice Department was interested in that.

And it maybe that now that he is deceased, more victims will be more willing to speak about who may have been in that chain to recruit them, to manage them, to pay them.

Allred also noted that as the search for evidence continues, it may turn up new names—and more proof.

"I understand there's a grand jury that has been looking into the circumstances of Mr. Epstein's death," she told us.

"There are many civil cases that are and will be ongoing, seeking discovery, seeking to find out the truth, and then there's the criminal investigation, which is probably more powerful than anything else, because the United States government has more resources than anyone else has.

"So I don't think any businessperson or celebrity or powerful man should rest easy and think, "Oh, well, there's not enough evidence."

"Well, maybe there is."

Indeed, two weeks after Epstein's death, authorities in France announced that they were launching their own investigation into sex crimes that might have occurred in Epstein's Paris home. In September 2019, they raided the posh apartment near the Arc de Triomphe, as well as the home and offices of his associate, modeling agent Jean-Luc Brunel. Brunel was named as a coconspirator in the unsealed Virginia Roberts Giuffre documents. He founded the MC2 modeling agency in 2005, reportedly with $1 million in seed money from Epstein.

Phone messages to Epstein from Brunel, found in Epstein's Palm Beach home and obtained by this team, suggest that Brunel may have connected Epstein with young models. The undated messages from Brunel to Epstein, as captured by Epstein's assistants, read:

He just did a good one . . . She spoke to me and said, "I love Jeffrey."

Jean-Luc "is in serious conversation about Alina's butt and he needs your precision."

"He has a teacher for you to teach you how to speak Russian. She is 2X8 years old not blonde. Lessons are free and you can have your 1st today if you call."

"Jean Luc spoke to the doctor about your symptoms. It's Bratislavian various. It can be cured but you have to move. It can cause atrophy of the muscle which can shorten your sex life."

The day we submitted this manuscript to the publisher, Brunel announced that he was willing to work with French prosecutors. On that day, his location was still unknown.

Homayra Sellier, the president of sex-trafficking-prevention organization Innocence in Danger, was behind the push for the investigation in France.

She explained:

We had women who came forward and they wanted to have juridical help to see what could be done with their testimonies, with their stories in France," she said, "in order to be a good citizen and to respect their duty as a mother, as a woman, as a citizen. So, they were guided to our juridical team, and they were forwarded at the discretion of the prosecutors and those who are doing the investigation.

In general terms, I believe that one of them concerns Mr. Epstein. Maybe also more, the other partners, or the other friends of his.

From my understanding, when he was operating in Paris, in France, it was very very very similar to the way he was operating in the rest of the world. He had friends who were recruiting young girls for modeling. Many of them were recruited to do those so-called massages, and they were going to his house. Then, once they were there . . . it was not a massage; at least, not for all of them.

I think his activity in France must have been quite big. I do think he had friends, maybe others who were putting him in touch with models.

Honestly, I think what happened in France is very, very, very similar to what happened in the US. You know this black book that was found or given or whatever? In that black book, there are apparently over sixty, seventy names of French people and there is a big number of women who are named as masseuses. But this is very similar to those who were going to his house in New York. So, it's the same operating system because it worked for him there, why would he change it?

According to Selliers, coconspirators around the globe could be exposed.

"I am not sure that the investigations will stop with the US and France," she said. "I had a call from some people who live in Belgium, and they were saying that people would like to expand the course of action in Belgium. Maybe then Germany. There were German models who were friends of Mr. Epstein, and who were going in his house, going to his parties. Even hosting parties with him."

Criminal investigations are not the only hope for future justice, however.

Several victims have already filed civil lawsuits in the hopes of getting closure—or cash—from Epstein's estate. Gloria Allred, Lisa Bloom, and Spencer Kuvin all represent victims continuing the fight, and each said that Epstein's coconspirators should not think for a second that they're off the hook.

"To the men in power, I hope they're afraid," Bloom said.

Allred, her mother, warned that more lawsuits are on the way:

Victims should know that they can file a civil lawsuit as a Jane Doe. That is our plan, at least for most if not all of our victims. We're going to be filing as Jane Does.

Members of the public do not need to know who they are, and they won't know who they are. Of course, a defendant has the right to know who's suing him, but the public does not need to know.

Shockingly, Epstein's coconspirators are trying to co-opt that strategy for their own devious devices. On September 3, 2019, an unnamed "John Doe" filed court papers begging a judge to block his name from being released in the event that Virginia Roberts Giuffre succeeded in unsealing more documents from her civil lawsuits.

The mysterious John admitted he didn't even know if he would be mentioned in the documents, but he would be taking no chances. His attorneys said they knew the explosive filings could include a "range of allegations of sexual acts involving the Plaintiff and non-parties to this litigation, some famous, some not; the identities of non-parties who either allegedly engaged in sexual acts with Plaintiff or who allegedly facilitated such acts." His attorneys did not confirm whether Doe could be considered famous or not.

Aside from Epstein's famous friends, his former staffers and "recruiters" like Ghislaine Maxwell are also now stalked by the searchlight as they hide out around the world.

One, Nadia Marcinkova (a.k.a. Nadia Marcinko), was yet another pretty young blonde in Epstein's roster of sex slaves. Brought from Yugoslavia at the age of sixteen, she quickly became one of Epstein's favorite companions.

During the Palm Beach investigation, a sixteen-year-old victim told cops that Epstein had forced her to perform oral sex on Marcinkova. Still, when police swooped in on Epstein, Marcinkova was spared. His non-prosecution agreement specifically named her as a coconspirator who would receive immunity from further prosecution, along with other alleged victims-turned-recruiters, Adriana Ross, and Sarah Kellen. (His assistant, Lesley Groff, was also named.)

That immunity agreement is only valid, however, in Southern Florida—not New York.

When asked about Marcinkova's role in the global sex ring, and whether she could be prosecuted, her attorneys told the *New York Times*: "Like other victims, Nadia Marcinko is and has been severely traumatized" and "needs time to process and make sense of what she has been through before she is able to speak out."

Marcinkova was unique among Epstein's girls in that she was able to attract attention outside of his inner circle. She trained as a pilot under his sponsorship, and built a huge YouTube following as the sassy and sexy "Global Girl." Now, other female pilots and aviation community members are disgusted to learn about what she may have witnessed or done.

"What Nadia Marcinko knows is a lot," said Florida air safety investigator Christine Negroni. "She has seen everything. When we talk about Jeffrey Epstein and the kind of information he took to the grave, he is not the only one who has that kind of information."

Negroni continued in an exclusive interview:

> She is also very, very aware of what happened in that house and his network of people, many of whom flew on his airplanes, many of whom have been reported to have participated in some of these activities.
>
> It's a tough spot for her to be in. I don't know: is she perpetrator? Is she victim? Reports suggest she came to the United States at the age of fourteen and that there were documents that suggested Epstein bought her from Slovakia at the age of fourteen.
>
> So it's very hard for me, and I hope for everyone, to be judgmental about a woman who may have facilitated these horrible crimes on young women when she herself might have been a victim. She seems to have made the best out of a bad situation. Whether that should be held against her I don't know.

She has a heck of a story to tell. The question is whether she'll tell it.

Of course, perhaps the only person who knows the whole story—from sex trafficking to espionage and everything in between—is Ghislaine Maxwell. Conveniently, at the time of this writing, she seems to have disappeared into thin air.

Days after Epstein's death, it was reported that she had been living in the quiet Massachusetts fishing village of Manchester-by-the-Sea, in the mansion of former boyfriend Scott Borgerson.

While Ghislaine was on the run, Epstein victim, Jennifer Araoz, filed a new lawsuit against her, alleging: "Maxwell participated with and assisted Epstein in maintaining and protecting his sex trafficking ring, ensuring that approximately three girls a day were made available to him."

But when reporters swarmed the Massachusetts seaside town, Ghislaine was already gone—if she'd ever even been there in the first place.

Our reporters went on the hunt in Europe and the United States. Then suddenly, there was a wholly unexpected twist: The *New York Post* published a photo of Ghislaine gazing defiantly at the camera while sitting at a Los Angeles In-N-Out, burger and fries in front of her.

Supposedly, the image had been taken by a lucky bystander who happened to recognize the woman who was then the world's most wanted.

But once you looked closer at the image, strange details began to emerge.

First, Ghislaine had a book in front of her: *The Book of Honor: The Secret Lives and Deaths of CIA Operatives*. It hardly seems like it could have been a coincidental choice. More likely, it was a pointed message to someone—or everyone.

Second, an advertisement in the background showed an ad for the movie *Good Boys*, a raunchy comedy in which preteens make R-rated sex jokes. The ad had been photoshopped into the image. The real ad at that location was for a local hospital.

There was also another clue that told family friend Laura Goldman that it was all a setup: "When I saw the picture of Ghislaine Maxwell at In-N-Out, I knew it was a fake immediately because she doesn't eat. Jeffrey liked thin women, so she starved herself to death. There was no way she was eating a hamburger and french fries!"

Later, a source would confirm to our team that the middleman—or middle woman, rather—who peddled the photo to the paper is a high-end Beverly Hills Realtor with property listings in Israel.

"I just talked to someone who texted with Ghislaine," Goldman revealed. "So she's definitely not in American witness protection. I think she's out of the country."

Goldman is sure of one thing: Someone has helped Ghislaine go deep, deep underground. Was it her spy handlers?

"If you know the Maxwell family, you know they're their own little team," Goldman said. "The seven siblings and Mrs. Maxwell supported each other completely.

"Ghislaine's sister Isabel has been married three times," Goldman said. "Her last husband also died mysteriously. They liked larger-than-life men."

Men, like their father, who had ties to international intelligence agencies.

***

Really, if you dig deep enough, the most powerful men of the twentieth century do have that one trait in common. While not all agents themselves, like Epstein, nearly without exception the leading figures of our time are connected by shadowy threads to the web of international intelligence, sexual blackmail, and the trafficking and abuse of children.

In a riveting series for MintPress.com, Chilean journalist Whitney Webb traced sexual blackmail practices back to 1920s and 1930s America, when leading liquor salesman Stan Rosenstiel hosted bugged "blackmail parties" with young boys for party favors. Rosenstiel invited the rich and powerful, for very specific reasons. Webb cites a Florida *Sun Sentinel* report that alleges

Rosentiel was once overheard saying "if the government ever brings pressure" against him or his pal, notorious mafioso Meyer Lansky, he'd use his recordings as blackmail.

During World War II, such techniques became more mainstream as the US intelligence community looked to mobsters and underworld kings for techniques to help them win against the Nazis. After the war, the wise guys' participation earned them a lifetime of "get out of jail free" cards.

Meanwhile, Lansky didn't limit himself to connections with and favors for the CIA. The shadowy character also worked with leading figures of the Mossad to launder money in the Middle East.

Supposedly, Lansky's own sexual blackmail ring was responsible for obtaining blackmail photos of FBI Director J. Edgar Hoover, leading to even more lenient treatment of Lansky and his associates throughout the 1950s and 1960s.

Although a victim himself, Hoover also was famous for collecting blackmail files on leading Americans, including the members of Camelot—the Kennedy family, and specifically President John F. Kennedy. Did he learn the tactic from America's original blackmailer, Rosenstiel? Hoover and the liquor baron were close friends, and Rosenstiel even donated $1 million to the J. Edgar Hoover Foundation.

Both men cultivated a mentorship of rising young politico Roy Cohn—Donald Trump's future mentor. Cohn became Senator Joseph McCarthy's adviser, and later worked with Ronald Reagan's administration. His meteoric rise through the ranks of the American elite, it seems, was due to his own "blackmail parties."

Rosenstiel's fourth wife, Susan Kaufman, later claimed to have attended one such party in 1968 at the Plaza Hotel in New York City. Kaufman said that in addition to Hoover himself in drag (going by the name "Mary") she saw young boys engaging in sexual behavior with Hoover, Cohn, and her then-husband.

Multiple reports claim that Cohn was unapologetic about hosting the gatherings, insisting that they were part of his anti-Communist crusade.

As with Epstein, Webb writes, many turned a blind eye to Cohn's activities. He was simply too connected, and had too much dirt, to take down.

Trump's former adviser Roger Stone explained: "Roy was not gay. He was a man who liked having sex with men. Gays were weak, effeminate. He always seemed to have these young blond boys around. It just wasn't discussed. He was interested in power and access."

Donald Trump would later buy Cohn's party palace, the Plaza, and host his own debaucherous bashes there throughout the 1980s and 1990s. Male model Andy Lucchesi told reporter Michael Gross that such parties were populated by "a lot of girls . . . 14, look 24. That's as juicy as I can get. I never asked how old they were. I just partook."

But Cohn's influence, like Epstein's, spanned both sides of the political aisle. His cousin, Dick Morris, was a close adviser to Bill Clinton. Cohn had connections in media, too: He was friends with FOX News head honcho Rupert Murdoch, and called Barbara Walters his "wife." His high school the pals turned friends for life included Si Newhouse Jr., Generoso Pope Jr. of the *National Enquirer*, and Richard Berlin, who owned Hearst. Many of Cohn's connections would later become close with Jeffrey Epstein as well.

Roy Cohn died in 1986, but sexual blackmail—including the trafficking of children—would continue to permeate the highest levels of American society.

In June 1989, George H. W. Bush and Barbara Bush were photographed visiting the Covenant House, a Catholic charity for homeless kids in Manhattan. It had been founded under the direction of Cohn's friend and frequent party guest, Cardinal Francis Spellman. Bush's Yale roommate, Robert Macauley, was on the organization's board. (His AmeriCares foundation funded Covenant House, while also working with the CIA to fund the Contras in South America. Like Epstein, Macauley lived in Palm Beach.)

Just weeks after the presidential pair's visit, Covenant House was the topic of a jaw-dropping exposé by the *New York Post*, which alleged that extensive child sex abuse had happened there.

That same year, the *Washington Post* reported that former NBC News correspondent Craig Spence had been caught running a D.C. child sex ring that provided underage sex slaves to powerful men in apartments that were bugged and rigged with security cameras. Even his parties, which hosted members of the Reagan and Bush administrations, had been bugged for gathering blackmail material. Spence even brought his prisoners to the White House for late-night encounters (not with the president).

Like Epstein, Spence often boasted to his friends and colleagues that he was working for the CIA. Also like Epstein, after his dirty deeds were exposed, Spence was found dead—supposedly by suicide.

***

For many, Epstein seems like a singular monster; at least, upon first encounter. A personification of evil that is deeper and darker than our society has ever known. Ultimately, however, the painful truth is that he was really nothing special.

Epstein's predecessors were many. Over the course of decades, none of them were stopped.

With Epstein gone, we are forced to face the sad fact that he will not be the historic first in this dark saga to face justice. As he joins the trail of heartbreak started by his predecessors, we are left to ask: Who are his contemporaries in sexual blackmail and the exploitation of children for espionage? And who are his successors?

Somewhere, it is certain, there are people who consider themselves to be the heirs to Epstein's darkest legacy: whether male or female, American or foreign, working for the CIA, MI6, or the Mossad.

Some we may suspect. Others will never raise the slightest hint of impropriety. Some we may even know.

It was not possible to stop Epstein, even with all of the stories we wrote and all of the brutal facts we exposed while he was living.

It may not even be possible to unravel his entire twisted life and network within the span of our lifetimes.

Dead men tell no tales, but we are compelled to tell them: stories of crimes, of conspiracies, of darkness.

In addition, we are compelled to listen: to those who missed the red flags, to victims whose lives were changed in an instant.

It is only in doing so that we can raise the slightest hope, the slightest chance, that we may ever stop the ones who wish to follow in Epstein's footsteps.

EPILOGUE

In the final days and hours of completing this book, disturbing new discoveries about the crimes and connections of Jeffrey Epstein continued to surface.

Even after reporting on him together for years, we found deeper and deeper layers of deception than we had ever known. As we gathered in team researching and writing sessions, the silence would be broken every few moments by one of us saying, "Oh my God."

There isn't time or space to connect and reveal every single detail we discovered. (Although, we'll probably spend the rest of our lives trying.) This book represents the best and most compelling reporting that we've ever done on Epstein and his cohorts. But this epilogue represents one of the spine-tingling stories that made our jaws drop when we discovered it—a story that could have been a book all on its own.

The summary is this: Donald Trump's personal fixer Michael Cohen and Jeffrey Epstein are *both* tied to a company called Reporty (now named Carbyne), which was then in the early stages of creating a new spy-like technology.

(Convicted felon Cohen plead guilty on August 21, 2018, to eight counts, including campaign finance violations, tax fraud, and bank fraud. Cohen said he violated campaign finance laws at the direction of Trump and "for the principal purpose of influencing" the 2016 presidential election. In November 2018, Cohen entered a second guilty plea for lying to a Senate committee about efforts to build a Trump Tower in Moscow. In December

2018, he was sentenced to three years in federal prison and ordered to pay a $50,000 fine.)

The stated purpose of Epstein and Cohen's business alliance in Carbyne was to help 911 callers by connecting the dispatch system to their cellphones' microphone, GPS, and camera, giving the dispatcher a live feed of the caller's surroundings. The obvious implication is that the same technology could easily be used to execute widespread spying and blackmail, to an extent the world has never before seen.

The explosive story of Carbyne's background was first published by reporters Zev Shalev and Tracie McElroy of Narativ.org.

In September 2017, Russian billionaires Viktor Vekselberg and Andrew Intrater bought 24 percent of Carbyne's most valuable stock options, through Intrater's company Columbus Nova.

(Intrater donated $250,000 to Trump's inauguration fund, and has already donated thousands to his 2020 campaign. His company also paid Cohen half a million dollars in "consulting fees." He was investigated by Robert Mueller's Special Counsel team.)

In 2015, the *Times of Israel* reported, Ehud Barak had formed a limited partnership company called Sum and bought all of Reporty's Series A stock—with most of the millions he needed to do so coming from Jeffrey Epstein. (It wasn't the first time he'd gotten millions thanks to Epstein. In 2004, Barak received about $2.4 million from Leslie Wexner's Wexner Foundation, where Epstein was both a trustee and major donor.)

Barak's cash infusion was enough to win him a seat as chairman of the board at Reporty, now Carbyne. The company is now based in Tel Aviv.

(In a twist that is sure to titillate Tom Brady haters, the Kraft Group is also a major investment source.)

In 2019, Carbyne partnered with Windbourne Consulting, a mysterious company that calls itself a "leader in public safety communications consulting and project management services to international, federal, state and local governments." Their headquarters is a mere five minutes away from the Pentagon.

Calling the technology "Smart911," Windbourne has already implemented Carbyne in the United States. Although, they may not want you to know about it.

A May 2017 Windbourne newsletter touted the platform's rollout in Michigan, announcing that the governor there had dedicated $2.2 million in grant funding to make the technology available to all residents. Anyone who put Smart911 on their phone and gave it access to their camera, mic, and GPS would get an eighteen-month subscription for free, the newsletter explained. The company also touted an oddly suspicious story from 2014, where a Michigan man who just happened to have Smart911 already installed was saved from a fire because of the app. The government and company encouraged all residents to download it.

But sometime after June 2019, in the weeks leading up to Epstein's arrest, that newsletter was wiped from the Windbourne website.

You may not have heard of it, but "Smart911" already has been implemented by local governments—and put on Americans' cellphones—in South Carolina, Ohio, Kentucky, Florida, Arkansas, New York, California, Massachusetts, Hawaii and more. According to Windbourne, Smart911 is in forty states at the time of this writing.

Newer versions of Smart911 reportedly also can access your personal photos, medical and health information, and other details.

The company insists, "It is *NOT* the goal of Smart911 to spy on you or share your information with anyone or any organization without cause."

The only consolation in the twisted story of Jeffrey Epstein may be that in the future, exploitative spies like him will probably become obsolete. Instead, we'll willingly gather intelligence on ourselves.

In 2020, who needs the classic honey trap when you've got the app?